JIM CROW
AMERICA

BOOKS BY EARL CONRAD

HARRIET TUBMAN: A BIOGRAPHY

JIM CROW AMERICA

JIM CROW AMERICA

BY EARL CONRAD

DUELL, SLOAN AND PEARCE

NEW YORK

TO MY FRIEND

DR. METZ T. P. LOCHARD

for his brilliant editorship of the Chicago Defender *and
his resultant contribution as a unifying force among Negro
and white Americans, and for his efforts in the development of the One World idea*

ACKNOWLEDGMENT

The critical and literary wisdom of my wife, Alyse Conrad, is written into every page of this book and I hereby acknowledge that. John Sengstacke, publisher of the Chicago Defender, cooperated with me throughout the summer of 1946, when this was written, and I am grateful. To them and to all those influences and persons which have helped mold me, and therefore this book, I say, "Salute and thanks."

E. C.

I AM a white war correspondent, and the war I'm reporting is going strong. I work in Harlem, but wear no battledress—just a reporter's everyday suit of clothes. Yet what I tell you about in this book is war correspondence just as surely as the dispatches that came from Tarawa and Normandy. In fact, my office is a kind of foxhole. This foxhole is the New York headquarters of the Chicago *Defender,* the big Negro newspaper. From it I look out on the great "racial fight" of America and, whenever I can, I take pot shots at "the enemy."

I report clashes over discrimination and segregation, interview big shots to get their views on Negro-white problems, investigate crimes and lies and political maneuvers. Often I have to hop a train to Washington, or take a plane to Alabama, to get at the source, to find out why something is happening. Whatever the assignment may be, I always have the feeling that it is all in the nature of a military skirmish, reconnaissance work for some great engagement that is bound to come. I know that I have changed sides—gone over to the black phalanx—and that I am ready for the big fight.

It is an axiom all over the world that the spirit of man is unconquerable. Man fights. What makes anyone in America think for an instant that Negro America isn't going to fight for its rights to manhood, security, decency, true equiform status? My story tells how that fight is progressing, who is in it, and who is being fought; how I got into it and how others are getting into it: it is a report of what *is* and a suggestion of what *ought to be*. It is a popular discussion of political issues you may or may not be familiar with, such as "race," "miscegenation," "gradualism versus immediacy," "the restrictive covenant," "integration versus segregation," and other facets of America's most complex social situation. Finally, it is a report on the explosive nature of the struggle of the darker Americans for fuller representation and participation in the complete pattern of national life.

In this story I think I have another kind of scoop, too, an inside story on what makes the Jim Crow situation what it is. Some time ago the city editor of the New York *Journal-American* laughed when I told him that the study of our national background, institutions, laws, beliefs—the examination of history books, old documents, records—could yield significant journalistic scoops, stories vitally related to the present. When I came to write this book I still believed in that idea, and therefore I assigned myself the added "undercover" task of digging up the background of Jim Crow, to see what light it could throw on the story of what is going on in the Negro-white world at this moment. As you will discover, I found a direct connection between the earliest slave ships out of England and the interracial clashes of today, between the misdeeds of a century ago and the misunderstandings of the present. In Jim Crow America the past is not dead, but very much alive. Maybe it will be writing headlines any day now.

—E. C.

[x

CONTENTS

JIM CROW
AMERICA

CHAPTER ONE

THE RAPE OF RECY TAYLOR

"I hope and trust God something will be done about it. . . . I can do nothing."
—MRS. RECY TAYLOR

IT WAS all so quiet on Sunday afternoon, January 7th, 1945, a mile outside of Abbeville, Alabama, in the pecan grove where I was standing. Beneath the warm sun, with the red clay sand underneath and the scrubby underbrush looking asleep for the winter, one would never have dreamed that on this patch of ground a young Negro woman had been raped five months before by six young white men. Someone pointed to the spot where Mrs. Recy Taylor, who was only twenty-four, and the mother of a two-year-old girl, had been attacked on the night of September 3rd, 1944.

Then I turned to look at Mrs. Taylor herself. The slight, copper-colored woman, with the large eyes, stood staring at the matted, haylike plot. She had come back to the scene with me, her father, daughter, and two others. It was the first time she had been there since the day after the raping. On that day she had shown the sheriff of Henry County the place where she had been attacked. Now, she and her family had taken me there—for someone had had a hunch.

3]

"Mrs. Taylor," I said, "you had better get back into the automobile."

As she reentered the car, I turned to the men and said, "Let's see if we can find anything."

Four of us hunted for a half hour. We were seeking evidence of the crime five months after it had happened, and we found it. We found the remains of six hygienic protectives which the rapists had used—not to protect the woman—but to protect themselves from one another. We found in excellent condition the packages that had contained the prophylactics, and other evidence. There was no doubt about the find. Recy Taylor had been kidnapped and taken to a secluded glade known to one of the attackers; it was no lover's lane, no public sparking spot; the evidence we had was evidence of only one incident that occurred there—probably one of the most shocking crimes committed in the recent history of an unregenerate South.

The South makes few apologies for its crimes of violence; it performs its rape and lynching pretty much for the world to see. The idea in back of its public crimes is "to let the Negro know," "to let the people see," to warn those who trespass on the sacred precincts of white supremacy. In this case, Alabama callousness and carelessness found no need to destroy the evidence of the crime. No sheriff foresaw any serious investigation, no attacker himself was so conscience-stricken or concerned as to feel it necessary to return to the scene. Our hunch was right.

We were feverish as we made the hunt, kicking and plunging around through the weeds, roots, stumps, and stones, making haste lest we be discovered. Even Mrs. Taylor was unable to restrain herself when she saw what we were about, and she got out of the car and helped us. Her child, Joyce Lee, tagged at her heels, moved about over the area where her mother had been so seriously attacked physically that she had been ruptured.

It was a perfect spot for the attack. On reaching the property we had quit a main road, traveled down a red-clay tractor path,

[4

then veered again into a small open glade sheltered from view. Trees in a great swerving group blocked the patch from the main road. An incline on the opposite side blocked out still another possible avenue of discovery. A fence separated this plot of unchivalric ground from a farm. Beyond the fence there stretched a long hill and at its peak one could see the outlines of a housetop. It was the house of the farmer on whose property we were now trespassing.

Although the glade had been sight-proof enough at night, when six Abbeville whites had done their work, this was daytime, and Sunday afternoon, and the owner of the property was out wandering around—and he saw us.

We had just about completed our search when the farmer, armed, with another man at his side, moved slowly toward us down the hillside. While he was still sixty yards away we could see that he was a robust, red-faced, middle-aged fellow—and we didn't like the look of the rifle in his hands. He was about halfway between the farmhouse and us when he called out, "What are you doing there?"

For a few seconds nobody in our party made any reply. Then Mrs. Taylor's father called out, "Looking for a five-dollar bill."

"Huhh? Five-dollar bill?" came the echoing curt, unbelieving reply. The farmer stared at me, the only white man in the group, here at the scene of a crime, here where he and everybody in Abbeville knew what had happened.

We continued, pretending innocence, to look for the bill.

"Well, you better find it and get out of here." He kept moving toward us, looking bigger, the rifle shining clearer.

Everyone entered the car. Nervously the driver backed out, rammed into the branches of a tree, barely averted going into a ditch, eased over a narrow, creaking bridge, returned to the main road, and righted the car.

After a swift drive we were at Abbeville again, sweeping into the small community of about two thousand people. We passed

5]

the large white courthouse looking majestic and solid, rolled down the main street where Sunday strollers glanced into store windows, then went down a hill to the outskirts of the town where three roads converged to a point. Nearby were five shacks like a row of gray sentinels, and in one of these Mr. and Mrs. Taylor and their daughter lived.

There were people in the cabin now, awaiting our return. They were curious about my call in the community, for the news of my arrival had spread rapidly among the Negroes. They were gathered in the main room which was bedroom, living room, and kitchen all in one. One corner held a large high bed, conceivably a hand-me-down from some "big house" of earlier days. The walls were decked out with pictures from magazines, and religious mottoes. A fireplace was alive with coals and heat, and some food was cooking.

The entire group was curious to hear something from me, it seemed, and I told them I had been sent there by a newly formed committee in New York, the Committee for Equal Justice for Recy Taylor. They listened attentively while I said that I represented thousands of whites North and South who were ashamed of what the Abbeville whites had done to Mrs. Taylor. We meant to bring the culprits to justice, to prevent such crimes from recurring, to do all that politics and pressure could do with the whole issue of white Southern treatment of black women.

I wasn't anxious to stay. The white townspeople would shortly know that a stranger was in town on the notorious rape case; it was possible I would be seized by the law or private hands if I lingered on; so I got to the point.

"Mrs. Taylor," I said, "you had better take your child and come to Montgomery with me. It's no longer safe for you here."

She stood next to me, the little girl at her skirts. "I can't," she answered. "My husband is away working now and I wouldn't want to go without him."

"He can follow," I suggested. "We can come back for him."

[6

"I have furniture. What will I do with that?"

"Forget about it, think of your life," I argued.

"I know I should," she went on. "I haven't been up into the town since it happened."

"Why not?" I asked.

"I'm afraid to. I'm afraid they'll kill me. They said they'd kill me if I told on them."

She *had* told on them; the news had spread; civic and religious groups had taken up her case; the knowledge of it had passed to the North; and the town knew that it was a center of attention, as Scottsboro, Alabama, had been once before.

When I saw that she wouldn't come away, I gave her some money in behalf of the Committee, told her to be ready to leave the place within two or three days, and then, with J.D., driver of the car that had brought me there, returned to Montgomery, Alabama, my base of operations.

A few days later Recy Taylor did arrive in Montgomery. She came with her husband and her child, but she did not stay there long. She drifted back into a rural area of the state where she remains to this day.

Doubtless Recy Taylor feels hatred for the State of Alabama that denied her justice, that twice failed to indict the rapists; perhaps she also bears a grievance against the white liberals North and South who abandoned her case and cause within a year. It would be natural enough for her to harbor such mistrust and hatred. Never was a woman more victimized by her county, state, and nation than this young mother. The liberals who fought her case for a time abandoned it because it seemed hopeless that the young men could be brought to justice. The legal machinery of Alabama made it possible for the rapists of Recy Taylor to go scot-free. Liberals were unable to budge the state, unable to find very much decency or assistance even in the churches of Alabama. For a time the Recy Taylor case was a symbol of "the Negro woman question"

7]

as it was a symbol of Alabama repression, but liberalism lost that fight.

It is a terrible thing, as I think back on it, to remember that woman and to realize that Alabama, the South, the United States "got away with it." I bumped into the power of white supremacy then and it was not a pretty thing to deal with. It is not a light-hearted enemy—and it is rooted in "thy rocks and rills, thy woods and templed hills."

In eight days in the state, part of the time under police surveillance, I had operated by plane, auto, and train between Birmingham, Abbeville, Montgomery, and Mobile. I had helped establish Recy Taylor Justice Committees in each of these places, had talked with CIO and Methodist leaders, and secured a promise from the Attorney General of Alabama that a new grand jury hearing would be called. I had helped organize an historic civil liberties meeting, attended by Negroes and whites, in a church in the very shadow of the State Capitol and had arranged Recy Taylor's flight from Abbeville.

My work done, I came from Alabama. I came from Alabama with no banjo on my knee, but the weeping of a black woman ringing in my ears.

For a time Alabama felt the impact of that case. Inside the state itself the big dailies and some individual voices called for a trial. The state received letters from white soldiers on foreign battlefields urging justice. For a short time the voice of an outraged black woman had power to stir a nation too long deaf to the cries of Negro women. In New York the great newspapers said nothing about this case. But the labor movement heard of it, and the Negro press reported it fully, hoping that white America would take Recy Taylor to heart.

I remember a talk with E. G. Jackson, the editor of the *Alabama Tribune,* a Negro weekly. It was Jackson, an energetic, middle-aged black man, with a militant approach, who had found the driver to take me to Abbeville. As the editor talked I couldn't fail to notice the lamplighted cubbyhole office he occupied. The office was in such contrast to the big *PM* building in New York where I had been working recently; and I thought too of the great Hearst building on South Street, Manhattan, where I had been a rewriteman. Down here a lone black man sought to write the truth, in the face of an officialdom that hounded his people and tolerated the mass rape of his women. There was a coal stove in the center of the room and it gave off plenty of heat; several worn desks were cluttered with papers; the walls were spattered with slogans, calendars, pasted newspaper clippings, a notary public sign, an insurance license. The floor was wooden and lumpy; the atmosphere compressed. Yet this was an office that fought the great Capitol about six blocks away.

"I hate to say this," he opened up hesitantly, "but we don't feel entirely secure in our women here."

"Why?"

"I don't say this in any criticism of our women at all, but rather in condemnation of the environment which has created all types of insecurity. We Negro men are helpless, powerless. The weight of hundreds of years hangs over us like so much iron and we would be superhuman if we alone could lift it off our shoulders."

He went on. "There is a certain amount of liaison between white men and Negro women wherein violence is not necessary. Whether for money, or from a desire to better themselves, or to free themselves of the poverty and powerlessness of the Negro man, many women are drawn into sex relationships with whites."

"How widespread would that be?" I inquired.

"That would be hard to say, but it is common rather than uncommon. But let the suspicion of a relationship between a Negro man and a white woman arise, and you will have your cue for a lynching."

"You need white help," I suggested.

"Yes, whites have imprisoned us, and whites may have to liberate us. We can cry out, and we do; we let them know our anguish, but we are outnumbered; we have no political power, no money, no real help, and the North does not care."

"But there are *some* liberals, aren't there?"

"Yes, there are some, perhaps a handful, but it is hard for them to act."

"But the church," I remonstrated. "Is there no help from there? I see churches in this town wherever I go."

He smiled and turned the wick higher in the lamp. "The church is not much different from the state. The church is as segregated as the residential areas." He paused and said wryly, *"Christ preaches white supremacy down here,* you know."

Then Jackson told me one horror tale after another, and he brought out newspapers to verify his stories. He told me that a frequent type of attack, difficult to prove, was that of white taxicab drivers who took Negro women into their cars, ostensibly to carry them to their destination, but first drove them outside the town and subjected them to attack. One news item told of Amanda Baker, a thirteen-year-old Negro girl, raped and poisoned and left to die by the side of a road. Jackson interrupted my reading to tell me that between 8000 and 14,000 complaints of Southern crimes had been made annually to the federal government since 1939. "In 1943 only thirty-one investigations were made and only three cases came to trial," he said angrily, and went on, "I blame the federal government for much that is rotten in the South."

"Can you answer this, Jackson?" I asked. "What is there in the locale of southeastern Alabama, in the town of Abbeville itself, in its background, that could make it possible for a thing like this to happen—for six young fellows to believe they could get away with this—and to be able, so far, to get away with it?"

"I can give you part of the answer," Jackson affirmed. "The answer lies partly in Henry County itself. Not so long ago this was virgin timber. The big sawmills came and brought hands. They also used convict labor. It was in the days before child labor laws or peonage laws. The stories about those sawmills, big con-

[10

cerns with no interest in the state but to get money, are not good. They cut the forest and moved on. Many people went with them . . . and the white people have kept toward the Negro the attitude of the sawmill owner to his convict labor. Henry County and its main town, Abbeville, has been off the main highways. There has been little money for schools; there is little or no industry. When you enter Henry County you go back a century, even a century behind the rest of Alabama."

"And the rest of the answer?"

Jackson tried to turn up the wick on the lamp, for the oil was burning low, and he mentioned that he chanced to have run out of oil, and we'd soon have to leave.

"The rest is history," he said. "It is the history of the South, of my people—and the degraded position occupied by our women."

When Jackson suggested that one would have to go back into history in order to understand fully why these young men felt they could get away with this act and escape punishment, he was absolutely right. To grasp it one has to take a look at the way white America has systematically degraded Negro womanhood ever since the slave trade.

The story of the Negro woman is, of course, identical with that of the Negro man except that there is a tremendous additional abuse in the experience of the black woman. I've heard this extra-special misuse of the black woman called "triple oppression." It is not a bad expression, and not at all untrue.

I would say that it all began in the year 1562 when Sir John Hawkins, sponsored by Queen Elizabeth of England, sailed off to Africa and captured the first boatload of African slaves. That trip, in a ship called, of all things, "The Jesus," might well have been the planting of the seed that flowered into the whole system of slave trading, plantation slavery, and modern Jim Crow. The one-and-three-quarters millions of Negro women working in the United States today under conditions of serfdom and caste can trace their "inheritance" back to "The Jesus" and a queen's desire for glory and wealth. That queen advised the traders not to carry off the Africans without their consent as that "would be detestable and call down the vengeance of Heaven upon the undertakers." But the slave trade developed not long afterward, with or without the vengeance of Heaven and the advice—however meant—of the Queen.

At the outset the Negro woman wasn't as desirable a slave as the young African man with stamina and strong sinews. The man could labor steadily and hard while there were times when the woman, producing children, could not produce sugar, cotton, rice, or tobacco. But in time the planters, despite their loss of labor through pregnancy of black women, found many uses for black women that made their enslavement as much a practical advantage as the capture of African men. For the trader a man might bring a higher price in the slave market, but the woman was easier to capture, and it was better to be sure of a small prize than none.

The classic pattern of Negro slavery was created by the state of Virginia. That state worked earliest and most diligently toward constructing the forms of chattel slavery. It was in Virginia that Negroes were first settled in America. There the Negro woman earliest came to be used as a field hand, concubine, household servant, mine worker, breeder, wet nurse, chattel slave.

In 1622 there were black women in Virginia, as the records attest. From the beginning the planters sought to make them an object of defilement, for in that year the burgesses established fines for fornicating with a Negro. And in 1630 Hugh Davis, a white man, was whipped "before an assembly of Negroes and others for abusing himself to the dishonor of God and shame of Christians by defiling his body in lying with a Negro, which fault he is to acknowledge next Sabbath day." This reveals how early in our national life Christianity and slavery went hand in hand, how the moral foundation of the nation was infected from the outset.

[12

Mostly, though, the record reveals the avarice of planters who sought to create out of the African a reservoir of gains beyond what could be obtained through their white indentured slaves. It was necessary for them to divide in order to rule, and color gave them the excuse. The difference in customs and language between the Africans and the white servants of English origin furnished planters with a weapon with which to belabor both groups of workers. Black and white could not be allowed to mingle or to marry because fraternization of the two groups would inevitably bring them to a unity of interest socially and economically. This would undermine the whole colonial structure. Kept apart, the groups remained enslaved.

With this enforced separation of the two laboring groups, America had started down the road that led to racism, civil war, and at last, in our time, the Negro-white situation that had caused the National Negro Congress to appeal for help to the United Nations Security Council.

The Negro woman's sex has always been used as an instrument for the economic subjugation of herself and her children. Her offspring by white men were, by law, "bound out" as slaves for a certain number of years. Negro women could be used carnally by white men but could make no legal claims for their own and their children's support. Legislation was frequently invoked against manumitted (freed) Negroes who married whites. Then both were "bound out," actually reenslaved, for a period of years. Such victimization struck forcibly, especially against Negro women. The extraordinary treatment to which they were subjected is reflected today in the broad social pattern, much as an "inherited characteristic" reveals itself in individuals: its principal form is the use of the Negro woman as a household or agricultural serf at subsistence wages.

Naturally all of her handicaps made the Negro woman less and less attractive as an object of association and friendship. The laws that separated white from black filled white men with fear also.

Disrespect went hand in hand with fear, and soon the woman of color "naturally" enjoyed a role as despised and degraded as the original power-seeking planters had wished.

The Negro woman was just as much a beast of burden as the black man. Often she was worked too hard to bear children, or at least, healthy children. Miscarriages were frequent; sterility, even, resulted from generally lowered standards of health. A woman in pregnancy received no more consideration from a planter than one of his plantation animals—and perhaps less. The planter was unconcerned, for as slavery intensified and the pace of labor increased planters reasoned that it was more profitable to exact great labor from a slave in a few intensive years of occupation, even if he or she died as a result, than to lighten the conditions of work.

Probably the meanest use of all to which the black woman was put in the slave period was her "employment" as a breeder. Slave-breeding became a major industry in Virginia, but it was the practice in other of the older Southern states too. When the soil of the Eastern states had been worn out and ceased to yield profitably, the South began an aggressive march westward. But it wasn't feasible for all of the planters to move westward; some decided to stay and fight it out on the great lands they owned. It was after the slave trade had been abolished in 1808 that the planters hit upon breeding of slaves for sale in the "internal slave market." In the years just before the Civil War, Virginia, Maryland, North Carolina, Kentucky, Tennessee, Missouri, and Delaware averaged a sale of about 80,000 slaves annually to the Southwestern states. These slaves had to be born and bred, and Negro women were encouraged to have as many children as possible. The mothers then saw their children taken away from them and sold. The internal slave trade worked great hardship on girls and women. The slaves were forced to make long migrations across the country, and these trips have been called as horrible as the original Middle Passage from Africa to the West Indies. And, of course,

[14

taking her part in these treks there was the black woman—"staggering along in the rear of the wagons at the close of a long day's march."

The Negro woman has had a hard time in politics, but because of her oppressed condition she has been a fighter. She has never willingly submitted to any of the forms of degradation. Negro women resisted capture in Africa, they joined in revolts on the slave galleys transporting them to the West, and they were even known to leap overboard, taking their children with them, rather than submit to slavery. In the colonial period revolts, and in the escapes of the Underground Railroad, they participated alongside their men.

Individual Negro women broke through the heavy bonds. In the eighteenth century there was Katy Ferguson, an educator and founder of the Sunday School system in America. Deborah Gannett, a soldier in the Revolutionary War, gave magnificent service. In the abolitionist period orators and fighters like Sojourner Truth, Frances Watkins Harper, and Harriet Tubman, distinguished themselves. As the woman suffrage movement gained impetus colored women like Mary Church Terrell and Mary Talbert played an active part, and today there is a vast army of "Mother" Bethunes in political, trade-union, and cultural life.

Negro women are not yet properly recognized in political parties, in labor organizations, in the general life of all communities. The Negro woman was discriminated against in the woman suffrage movement. Even Negro men, influenced often by the notions of male supremacy which circulate widely among white men, reflect similar attitudes toward the Negro woman. Thus the black woman has been hemmed in on all sides.

To me the amazing thing about the tradition of Southern white male treatment of Negro womanhood is its long history of escape from responsibility. So widespread and varied have been the crimes against the black woman that, apparently, the Negro people and their white allies have been unable to take hold of this issue and

15]

fight it out. Whether because the caste system has been so power-ful, and remains so powerful, or because anti-Jim Crow forces have never been efficiently mobilized, the truth is that the age-old misuse of the Negro woman has not had its proper hearing in American courts and American minds.

The abuse of the Negro woman in her perennial role as a work-horse, is one of America's greatest crimes. It is only a short step from her debasement as a serf in field and home to her mass rape by six young men in an Alabama meadow. The violence done to Recy Taylor goes back to the time when the slave ships packed their holds with the women and children of Africa. The rapists of Alabama followed an age-old pattern which the South hesitates to alter, and the North too much condones. As a consequence the economic and democratic development of the South and of all America has been held back, and the nation is put to shame throughout the world. In Africa, China, India—everywhere, men can say and they are saying, "Part of America is feudal. Part of one of the most advanced nations is the most backward section, of the world."

When I was in the South on the Taylor case I learned that vio-lence as a political principle of living and a policy of individual officials, even as a matter of state policy, merits formal discussion among white Southerners. I heard personalities in and out of the state machinery of Alabama discussed as follows, "Soandso believes in violence," or "He tends to believe in violence," or "He is against violence." I found that *the principle of violence* was discussed there as casually as people in the North might discuss craft union-ism versus industrial unionism, or nationalism versus international cooperation. Later, when I reported what I had heard to Dr. Metz Lochard, the Negro editor of the Chicago *Defender,* he said, "Only a white man could have heard such a conversation. I doubt whether a Negro would be permitted to hear such a discussion, or whether a Negro ever has heard such."

It is possible that in the polar relationship of the white man and the Negro woman lies the weakest link in the American system. Here are the two most remote positions: on one side, white male supremacy and economic power, on the other, black female degradation and poverty. The future may, in large measure, rest on how our country approaches and resolves that disparity.

CHAPTER TWO

TWENTY-FIVE CENTS

The Economics of Jim Crow

CALL the barrier between black and white "America's Chinese Wall," or "the caste system," or "the test of democracy." Whatever one's attitude, one must acknowledge that since the onset of World War II this issue has become pivotal in domestic politics and national thinking. The war against the Nazi master-race theory compelled us to look ashamedly at our own *fait accompli* of a master-race way of life.

Negro America blew up over the contradiction of having to fight racism abroad and live under it at home. A great wartime riot occurred in Harlem, and was denounced by the New York press as "the most vicious riot in Harlem's history," while what should have been excoriated, our system of legalized racism, went generally unmentioned. Negroes were segregated in the United States armed services. Not even the Nazis had dreamed up such an idea! Men got into uniforms, traveled, started thinking. New organizations formed and went into motion as political allies of the Negro. Reflecting the political upsurge, plays came to Broadway; a new, a modern anti-slavery literature issued from the presses; a few liberal dailies gave emphasis to the position of the Negro.

But it wasn't all so sudden. The process of the breakup of separate relations between the groups had been going on since the 1929 crash. Labor organizations early pressed the issue of Negro rights; white and black workers on assembly lines became acquainted. Millions of Negroes escaped northward out of the oppressive white dictatorship down below. Whites looked across the street at their new neighbors—and the gulfs stood—or the gulfs tottered—but the thinking went on and on. Church leaders came to grips with their conscience and took their stand. Small circles of black and white, like islands in a great sea, fraternized in the big cities. There were covert and open sex relationships of black and white; marriages too. Men and women were finding their way across lines, smashing down the centuries-old schism. It wasn't easy. They had to fight to get closer.

It took me fourteen years, fourteen years of fighting myself and others, of associating with Negroes—reading, thinking, writing—before I found myself in Harlem as a newspaperman. It was like moving through a fog, or hacking steadily at a prison wall, or climbing a formidable mountain.

How many others are now groping through the fog, hacking at the wall, pounding up the mountain? I don't know, but I know that this story, the experience of millions of whites struggling to open their eyes and hearts to the darker brother, is one of the great phenomena of this period. Now I shall tell how it all began for me, which is probably something like the beginning for many others. . . .

Older people will recall the amusement with which the formation of the Kiwanis Club was greeted by many observers in the Sinclair Lewis generation. The Kiwanis announced that they were very different from the Rotary Club. The Rotary Club admitted to membership in each of its local chapters one representative of each business in the community; the Kiwanis, a democratic organization, planned to take in two representatives of each business.

Something of that same kind of naivete marks the supremacist South, I found, when I was down there for the first time in 1932.

"We do not believe in enslaving Jews," said a white Southerner to me, very solemnly, and with a great air of liberalism, "because Jews are white people and no white people should enslave any other white people. Niggers, that's different."

I had been in Orlando, Florida, only a few weeks, long enough to become fascinated with its pretty lakes, palm-lined streets (in the white quarters of the town), its Spanish fern hanging grace-fully—if vermin-laden—from the wide-spreading trees, its modern buildings and well-cared-for commercial avenues, when the social contradictions began to bedevil me. For one thing, the statues in the city parks, with their curious inscriptions, were puzzling. Each said something bitter, which ran about like this: "The Daughters of the Confederacy will not soon forget their sacrifices in the War Between the States. A day of reckoning will come." If not exactly in these words, then in others that revealed a nostalgia for the days of slavery, that threatened the North, that showed an undying determination to turn the clock back and put the Negro "in his place." Monument after monument carried such inscrip-tions. Nothing subtle, nothing poetic, nothing but the threat of another civil war—come the proper time.

I found no originality in the expressions of supremacy, but a deliberate uniformity, a credo. It was as if everybody had been trained to the use of the same model Winchester rifle. "We un-derstand the Negroes," they said. "We understand them." Each Southerner with the supremacist position said it just that way. "Why, if you give them an inch, they'll push you off the sidewalk." You could hear this four or five times a day without inviting it. It was as if it had been taught in the school, and the home, as if it had been written on a political banner strung between buildings on the main street. The attitudes of the supremacist South had been formalized, frozen, set. When they said, "The Negro has his place," and they said it all day to themselves, to one another, to all

[20

Northerners, and to Negroes, it was as organic and casual as repeating the slogan, "Orlando: The City Beautiful." The same insults, tone, language everywhere, like a steady rainfall: "They're dirty," "They're ignorant," "They're lazy," "They're inferior." Each comforting the other with the same elementary expletives, each shielding himself, his community, and the sectional past, behind the same iron screen. The words, the replies, the attitudes came as readily from the citizens of Orlando, with the same naturalness and inevitability, as the cackle comes from the rooster at daybreak.

I had come to the city beautiful for a vacation and a sightseeing tour, and within a few weeks I was troubled, baffled, angry. What were they trying to defend? What were they trying to make themselves and others believe? What was up, anyway? Was it only Negro America that was suffering from this? The thing was so enormous that one had to look for an explanation. What were its roots? Why was the belief in white supremacy in the South such a virulent and ubiquitous thing? There must be a reason. Something must have happened. *What?*

Perplexed, I simply moved about the community and watched the great contradiction at play. . . .

It played, too, it played all day and all night, like the Gulf breeze that never lay quiet. Black and white mixed in a dangerous interplay at all times. Social and economic codes stumbled and blinked. Tunes kept going through my mind, the traditional songs of Dixie, the nostalgic melodies of the swampland, "Sweet Georgia Brown," "Back Home in Tennessee," "Mississippi," "By the Tamiami Trail." In the North magnolia had seemed so inviting; the South was a melodic paradise, its scenes joyful and warm and human, its peaches beauties. All the stuff and nonsense of Tinpan Alley went through my head like an earache. In a week or two the songs went out of my system, and they have never returned. I saw too much, too much that made me sink inwardly, ever to be lulled again by a Phil Harris musical reminiscence of the Southland, or a Jolson warble of bluebirds and mammies.

Three Orlandoans sought my opinion of a new organization they planned, the Silver Riders. I examined their program. The key to it was a statement that the Negro was providing sharp economic competition for white workers. Hence, white employers and white workers should band together. "Have you been told your plan contains features such as Mussolini endorses in his own program?" I asked. They hadn't. What puzzled me for a long time afterward was their denial that their program was fascist. "It's strictly Southern," they said. That explains why Bilbo and Talmadge, for example, are widely regarded in the South as "strictly Southern" rather than fascist.

A liberal apologist for the Southern system denied that chain gangs were so very bad. At the time Robert Burns, a fugitive from a Georgia chain gang, had written a book focusing attention on the practice of chaining prisoners, and the South was uncomfortable. My friend said he could arrange for me to get on a chain gang for thirty days just to test it out, if I were willing. He insisted I'd find it wasn't so bad. I passed up this splendid opportunity.

I talked with a farmer who zealously guarded the orange trees on his plantation. Stealing an orange in Florida was a crime virtually punishable by death, I was told by a number of Floridians. "Let me catch a nigger swiping one of my oranges, I'll plug him," said one farmer to me. Said another, "When I drive my car and I see a nigger crossing the street I don't put my foot on no brake. I'd as soon run him down as I would a rabbit." Said another, "If a nigger don't get off the sidewalk and step onto the curb when I come along I curse him out and I'd as soon kill him." It was a refrain, like steady tropic rain, wherever I went. No insult was too base, no contempt sufficiently expressive, no action too ugly to prove white superiority.

Over the years as I have worked at this question, this Negro question, I guess that what I have tried to do, as much as anything, has been to wipe out of my mind and system the remembered sights of those ten weeks in Orlando. Sometimes I wonder how

I could have seen so much, or why I saw so much, why I stayed there so long. There was the old, white-haired Negro who, coming down the street a half-block away, stopped still and held out his hand for a coin, then stepped off the sidewalk in a wide circle of respect, and just stood there looking at me wearily and hopefully till I drew alongside and dropped that coin in his palm. Or the two young Negro men, in tatters, seated on a park bench, each ripping apart a loaf of bread, just ripping it apart and stuffing it down to quell fierce hunger, and the look of irritation they gave me when I stopped in my tracks, shocked to behold the sight. Or the five-year-old white boy who stood guard while two middle-aged Negro men fixed a lawn: the look of power on that little boy's face, and the look of humiliation on the faces of those two men who glanced at me with their hopelessness and shame. Then I saw how the South inculcates its supremacy. It says, "Johnny boy, you watch those two niggers while they work. Let me know if they go too slow."

When I mildly suggested to a young woman there that it was a little bit unfair, she warned me, "Listen, you better not go around making such misstatements. You might get into trouble. You might just get told by someone to catch a train and get out of here in a hurry." When I wanted to know why, and wasn't it America here, and wasn't there such a thing as free speech especially when it concerned people's rights, the answer was: "This is America, all right, but this is the South, my friend. You better do as the Romans do."

I chummed around with a couple of white boys from Georgia. One of them drove a truck, and he was proud to be a Culpeper, a Virginia Culpeper; he was going to show me Florida and teach me how to treat "niggers." I accepted his invitation to take a ride "down through the country," as he put it. When I climbed onto the seat of the truck, I suddenly saw a little colored boy, a lean kid of twelve or thirteen, open a wooden slab on the side of the seat and crawl inside. In a jiffy he was lying beneath the seat, beneath me, where the tools lay, and I could hear his body rattling the tools as he tried to make himself comfortable upon them.

"That's Sammy, my boy," explained Culpeper. "He carries crates into the stores for me."

"Why don't you let him ride with the produce on the back of the truck? He'll suffocate in the tool box."

"Oh, no, he won't. He likes it there. He likes to be right underneath me. We both like it." Culpeper was smiling, giving the truck the gas, and we were moving, with a living, human little boy jammed into the toolbox of a seat.

I rode seven or eight hours that day in that truck and watched the boy jump in and out of that toolbox, and never heard him mutter a word, and I hated to say it to myself but I kept thinking, "Like a dog." It was only years later that I realized how terribly dependent this peon was upon that master and upon that job. That night I saw Culpeper generously drop a quarter into the outstretched palm of the silent boy, who then ran off to eat.

The whole thing fascinated me. The snake nature of white supremacy drew me deeper into its eyes and I even lived with Culpeper and his friend for three weeks to see what more there was to see. It was their experiment with a Yankee and mine with "the rebels." It lasted three weeks, this sharing of the apartment, until the day when they robbed a Negro washwoman of twenty-five cents. She had done an enormous laundry, a laundry that, at that time, even in the South was a four-dollar wash, though her agreed price was a dollar and seventy-five cents. And then, on the day when she trundled up the staircase with the huge laundry on her back and put it down, Culpeper advanced on her and said, "Here's a dollar and a half. That's all it's worth."

I argued with him and the other chap, telling them to pay her what they said they would pay her. I said I would pay the other quarter myself. They wouldn't allow it. They stood between her and me. She was watching the drama, knowing something curious was going on, but hating us all uniformly, and she was asking for her extra quarter and telling us how much the soap alone cost. Now their voices rose sharply and they told her to be gone; she turned and started down the stairs and the daring whisper, "Sons of bitches," came back up the stairs. Culpeper made a rush for the door, calling her a "nigger bastard" and yelling he'd throw her down the stairs, but his sister blocked his path and he quieted down. Right after this our experiment broke up, our apartment folded. I went my way and they went theirs.

There was the evening I spent at a white working-class home on the outskirts of Orlando and the woman of the house, hearing I was from the North, gave me the song of the South: how, even though they worked for her, they were dirty; even though they cared for her child, they were diseased; even though they got only three dollars a week, they were lazy; and the other stock sayings. I listened as long as I could and I said: "If they're dirty why do you let them work in your house? If they're diseased why do you let them raise your child? If they're lazy why don't you hire people who aren't lazy?" She came back with a strange reply, "You wouldn't want Japanese to cook for you and work for you and take care of your house, would you?" It was long before anybody in the country, certainly the general public, was concerned about Japan, and I answered, "The Japanese? No. Why do you have to have Japanese, or Negro, or anyone else? Can't you do the work yourself?" Then a chair that she picked up came hurtling across the room; it hit me in the elbow and it hurt.

Years afterward I realized that I had hit upon the fundamental nature of the question. I had hit the woman in her economic breast and she had replied as the South usually replies, *with force*.

Everywhere I went there were overtones of violence. Always the suggestion of it, the warning of it, and finally the deed. The rattler was the symbol of the Southern spirit. The Southern white woman—those who were unregeneratively supremacist, at least— were as brutish as their men. Force and violence: this was the credo and it dogged me all over "the city beautiful" until the night

25

when I heard the honking of a horn outside my rooming house and a friend called me outside. She was in haste, and she gave me a warning, saying: "I think you better get out of town. My husband is a Klansman. They have been talking about you for weeks. They have just had a meeting about you. You better get out or something will happen."

"What will happen?" I asked.

"I don't know. Maybe tar. Maybe a ride into the country. Please get out—tonight."

I got out of the beautiful city that night.

Everybody has heard the old bromide, "It's not the cash, it's the principle of the thing." Cash and principle are sometimes separate, but often identical. In the South the principle of the thing is the cash. In fact, there is no other principle of living which guides the supremacist so much as that of cash. As Jesus said, "Where a man's treasure is there shall be his heart also." It isn't a far cry from cash to caste; I guess they are the same, too.

A number of years passed before I concluded that those Southern boys who were willing to throw a Negro woman down a staircase for twenty-five cents were interested solely in hanging onto that quarter. Incidentally they were willing to show me how they handled the Negro and how they kept themselves on the economic top, but initiating me into the beauties of the Southern economy was only a secondary motive. They were out to save two-bits. Two-bits was two-bits. The fracas with that woman over twenty-five pennies would have occurred even if I hadn't been there.

I don't mean to be too harsh on those Southern lads, at least no harsher on them than they were on that woman. After all, they inherited their economy, they did not create it. Their grandfathers took everything from the slave—his labor and his life—and apparently it takes time for a nation's economy to get regulated along some kind of a line approximating decency. It is taking the South a very long time, but that will come too.

TWENTY-FIVE CENTS

These young fellows hadn't partaken of the slave trade, they hadn't run plantations before the Civil War, they hadn't taken part in the Klan restoration of supremacist rule in the 1870's and 1880's. It would be unfair to blame them for their historical past. It would be blind to say that they had made themselves into the image of the brutes that they were. It was history that had made them so. Greed had come to America, along with democracy, and greed was built into the hearts and minds of many millions of whites who were the products of the past, not its creators.

I saw that the generation of today in the Southland had inherited the warped hangovers of slavery, and if one were weak or inclined to apologize, one could say he was sorry for them, that their plight was pathetic, and he could walk out on the question. Apparently that was just what America had been doing for a long time. But it was too simple. This was to ignore responsibility for revising the direction of today's history. These young men had to come to their senses, or to be brought to their senses. Sorrow and pathos were not enough, either for the white or the black. There is no future for the South in pitying it or in pitying itself.

It should not seem so far-fetched that the key to understanding the South, and perhaps our whole history as it relates to the Negro, is to be found in twenty-five cents. That, indeed, is a large sum. I daresay the South's many-thousand toll of lynchings can show a number committed for even smaller sums. I know of one Reconstruction period murder committed during an argument over a sack of ashes which, I imagine, wasn't worth more than a quarter of a cent.

The issue comes down to pennies, then, and so it has been since the time when slave traders marched into Africa, handed out a few bottles of rum, and walked off with a hundred or so human commodities. The profit then was enormous. Since free labor conquered the South the plantation owners have had to calculate profits on a penny basis rather than enjoy the exorbitant profits of an exorbitant era. But whether in the slave trade, on the slave plantation, or in the mixed slave-feudal-free labor economy of the South today, the Negro remains a special source for an extraordinary profit. To say that the Negro represents a special and traditional source of extra income to the business and propertied classes of America, especially in the South, may seem an oversimplification of the economics of Jim Crow, but it does express and hit at the fundamental fact.

Twenty-five cents in the hands of two white men is twenty-five cents less in the hands of a black laundress. Magnify that in terms of the economic process intensively at work in all the Southern states, and almost as sharply operative in the North, and you put an arrow through the heart of Jim Crow. Robert C. Weaver, a Negro economist, has pointed out that animosity between white and Negro was inevitable during the slave period once a concept of status based on race and color was introduced. It was extremely useful for those who benefited from slavery because it confused an economic issue with a racial one. With slavery abolished, a color occupational system has been substituted. "It serves to conceal the basic nature of economic problems and cover them with color situations."

I know now that the twenty-five-cent robbery by two young white men in Orlando in 1932 was cut out of the same cloth, colored red, white, and blue, from which was scissored the rape of a black woman in 1944 by six young men in an adjoining state, that each of these incidents was part of a pattern, or as I prefer to call it, an historically evolved *system*. This system contains many sides, facets, processes, movements, and not until we report on its various tentacles can we get a picture of the octopus called Jim Crow.

CHAPTER THREE

BLACK AND WHITE LABOR

"The CIO is teaching the church the Christianity that the church in practice ought to reveal to the world."

—BISHOP G. BROMLEY OXNAM

O F ALL the false allegations the Negro American has had to face the one that has intrigued me most has been that of his "laziness." This misconception doubtless has its origin in the South, and, like all other miscomprehensions of the Negro's reactions, it stems from the early slave plantation use of the black man's productivity. Here is a people which, historically, has borne much of the burden of the nation's labor and growth; certainly for the first two centuries of our history the Negro was the national ox. Then there is the fantastic anomaly of the Negro's being accused of laziness. The Negro creates the wealth of a Confederacy, but he won't work! He remains to this day a major agricultural worker and producer of food for white Americans but, say his employers, he dawdles, he is lazy. One hears that everywhere in the South and perhaps just as widely in the North. Mostly this slander comes from individuals who directly employ Negroes, while they themselves do no maintenance work, carry no boxes, pitch no hay, drive no trucks, run no elevators, clean no hotel rooms, fix no dinners.

Two years after I had been in the South I came to New York and it was there, in Washington Market, the produce terminal of the metropolitan area, that I saw the myth of the "lazy Negro" exploded before my eyes.

A chain of developments that may have begun with the eye-opening sights of Florida led me to help in the organization of truckdrivers and porters working in the market. That was a period when many young people were becoming interested in labor and social outlooks. The Scottsboro Case rang through the land, Angelo Herndon was trapped in a jail in Dixie, the breadlines were hundreds deep at a dozen places in Manhattan. Newspapermen were organizing the Newspaper Guild. I had been a newspaperman since the age of fifteen, and came to New York looking for work. Jobs were infrequent and paid poorly, and when some of my acquaintances pointed out to me that my social insecurity stemmed in good part from the unorganized nature of the employed and the unemployed, I became interested in Labor.

I found myself helping teamsters, chauffeurs, and porters organize "a rank-and-file movement" within a union covering the workers in the produce market. It was when I went into the market, usually at night, to distribute literature and make contact with the employees, that I saw thousands of Negroes laboring there—I might even say slaving—as porters, and learned that owing to their presence in large numbers the market situation rated as "complicated."

A lazy man, white or black, wouldn't have lasted ten minutes in Washington Market. I can still see that place as I saw it for the first time about a decade ago. It is an area of narrow streets, about fifteen blocks long and three or four blocks deep. At midnight, which was the time when I was usually there, the scene looked and sounded like a local battlefield in a civil war. The streets, none wider than thirty or thirty-five feet, were packed with motor and horse-drawn trucks, and the trucks were jammed in the avenues like the produce in one of the crates they carried. The wheeled vans plunged through the slim lanes, in a constant motorized volley of sound. One-ton trucks, horse-drawn wagons, huge trailers, and boxlike monsters of the American Railway Express jabbed and darted, each to get to a certain shop, to turn a corner, to get into or out of the market. The widespread heave and motion in the streets produced a din like some low-grade type of guerrilla warfare. Brakes screeched, horns fired, and tires ripped out earsplitting bursts; while in the midst of it all, men, black and white, labored.

From midnight on, the market is ablaze with illumination; it is brighter than Broadway's theatre district, many times as noisy, and many times more dramatic than most plays showing there. The light comes from strings of electric bulbs in the streets, from floods of electric glare pouring out of fruit and produce shops, and from the headlights of automobiles.

The market labor on any one night feeds the metropolitan area the following day. The traffic is that of fruit and produce entering the city from throughout the North, East, and South. The food is sold, trucked, portered, selected, trimmed, ordered, discarded, and otherwise prepared or handled for delivery to the stores, restaurants, and hotels of the city.

Drivers, helpers, porters, businessmen, union organizers, salesmen, peddlers, grocers, cops, thugs mingle all night in a terrific traffic snarl that unwinds itself each dawn. There is over all a smell, faintly of the farm, faintly of a garbage dump. The tropic fragrance of bananas, coconuts, and pomegranates mingles with the perfumes of Northern-grown apples and a hundred other products.

Although the truckdrivers maintained that their job was the hardest, the porters, most of whom were Negro, swore that portering was the toughest work in the world. About two thousand of the latter crowded the sidewalks, passed in and out of the stores constantly carrying on their shoulders crates laden with produce. One man might be pushing a handcart carrying five hundred pounds of produce. Another would shoulder a crate of foodstuffs weighing eighty or a hundred pounds.

What convinced me once and for all of the eagerness of the Negro man to be a useful citizen, to earn his living honestly, to be willing to work reasonably and even unreasonably to that end, was the sight of a mass of reserve workers who hung about the market waiting for the opportunity to get a few hours of part-time work. This very group also constituted the principal issue in the market's labor question, just as the unemployed, nationally, signified the great "problem" of private enterprise. The Washington Market businessmen welcomed this extra labor supply that paraded through its streets nightly, stopping at each fruit and produce shop seeking work loading or unloading a truck. These black workers would carry a ton or so of produce from a truck into a shop or from a shop out to a waiting truck for a half-dollar. It was backbreaking labor, yet hundreds of Negro workmen, who may have had every provocation in the world to take up rackets, crime, and revolt, preferred to fight it out as workingmen, to take their chance in a place where cops hounded them, white unionists hated them, and businessmen treated them as contemptuously as plantation owners treated their slaves.

I would look at these men and marvel at their stoicism in the face of such great odds. As long as they remained outside the union, and as long as the union existed on paper only and wasn't allowed to function, the businessmen could use these reserve laborers to force down the salaries of the unionized workers and keep labor competition extremely active in the market. The lower the cost of loading and unloading trucks, the greater the profits from the sale of produce to restaurants, hotels, food shops. Black labor in the market, reserve labor, was one of the more important means by which the produce houses made their profits.

New Yorkers, the next morning, eating the fruit that was handled in the market the night before, never realized that Negro scab labor, a basis of produce merchants' extra profits, helped so

[32

much in determining prices. Nor could they know how this element of reserve labor disintegrated the working conditions of thousands of unionized workers, Negro and white.

Deep in the Southland black workers who cultivated much of the agricultural product that came into the market were having a battle with the orchard owners and landholders of their region. Up North, in the last handling process of this produce, black labor was still being used to squeeze out a final bit of profit for another, a Northern, business class. Here was a kind of North-South axis of unorganized Negro labor exploited as a means of special profit, and one could see the whole process working out as smoothly as a newsreel before one's eyes.

This segment of reserve labor tramped through the market at all hours of the night. They were gathered around bonfires at street corners on winter nights to keep from freezing to death. The fires blazed from steel trash cans at each corner. The men burned paper, wood, kerosene, anything, so that a half-dozen of them could hug the fire and keep warm against the night's sharp cold while they waited—often vainly—for the signal from some merchant to go to work on a truck. Winter and summer, day and night, many of them slept in the market. On the darkened side streets of the adjoining butter and egg market, on Greenwich Street, which operated by day, and was closed at night, these men lay on doorsteps and on ramps leading into the establishments.

The cops chased them from one end of the market to the other, yet were under strict orders not to drive them out of the market altogether. "Keep them moving, but keep them here," was the directive.

Migrants, who came to New York from Detroit or Chicago (and they had come before then from Birmingham or some other Southtown)—this corps of reserve labor—huddled in the streets in their scant clothes, lean bodies attesting their struggle. Their plight symbolized, for me, the plight and the question of Negroes everywhere. It was, too, the problem of Negroes who had to work

33]

with whites, of whites who had to work with Negroes, of men black and white seeking to get work, competing for it.

They hung about ready to undersell the labor of the union people on the job, ready to compete with black or white employed, and protected by the employers, the police, and the corrupt union leadership. "If it wasn't for the colored," said the white unionists to me, "we wouldn't have any trouble in the market. There'd be enough work. We'd get the pay promised us in the contract. But they use these guys against us." I would answer, "What you've got to do is get these fellows into the union with you as an unemployed section available for full- or part-time work." They would answer, "Yeah, but the union don't call meetings. What are we going to do?" And I'd say, "Get a petition going, let a delegation bring the petition to the union hall and give it to Buck Thompson." (Thompson was the chairman of Local 202 of the Brotherhood of Teamsters, Chauffeurs, Stablemen, and Helpers, with jurisdiction over the markets.) Then they would say, "Yeah, sign a petition and get your brains beat out like Charley Wurtzl. Or go see Buck Thompson and get hit over the head with an iron bar like Pete Mago." Their replies were the truth. There was terror in the market, minor terror to be sure, but it was there, as a threat to the organized to keep quiet or be mauled around by goons. The businessmen liked it that way and everybody understood that the union chiefs took money from the businessmen's organizations in the market in return for denying meetings to their membership and beating up an occasional militant worker.

Naturally the Negro, as a reserve laborer, was resented by the organized men. The Negro rated as a scab and strikebreaker. But when a union failed to organize them and Negroes needed a dollar or two a day to live, what were they to do? They could only hang around and be hated, and be called upon occasionally to load or unload a truck for a half-dollar or a dollar. If they got two trucks a night to handle they were lucky. If, after staying out in that freezing weather all night, they came away in the morning with

[34

a dollar in their pocket it was a good night's income. Many a reserve worker went through the night without getting work, and he had to mooch a dime for coffee and doughnuts from a fellow Negro porter, or nickel carfare to get back to Harlem.

I had two years of that, two winters of it, night after night, in the cold of Manhattan's waterfront. The wind, blowing in from the west, crossed the Hudson River, caught up fierceness from the cold water, and struck against the waterfront. It swept past the docks and poured into West Street, filling this broad, darkened avenue with its wintry gift, and threshed into the lighted lanes. By two o'clock in the morning the temperature would be down to the bottom; and the market, a region not more than a third of a mile long and a few hundred feet deep, raged with a shivery fury—and black and white labor, employed and unemployed, raged in the same way.

The gusts of cold river wind were no help to the several thousand porters as they piloted their burdened handtrucks across the sidewalks from stores to trucks, and back again. The word "porter" is a mild and inexpressive term for their work. Negro and white bent equally under this performance; each wore out with the same speed.

Our persistent efforts finally made an impact in the market. After a time the union meetings become more frequent, a better element took leadership of the local, and my work there came to an end.

This was where I learned how crucial the "Negro question" was. It wasn't long before I saw that it was essentially a question in exploitative economy. The question was: "What are we going to do to give the Negro a chance to be a full partner in the America he has helped build?" Down there in the market, as elsewhere, he hadn't been given that chance. He had been used, as he has always been used, for the ends of some white men. He had been used by the employers for his cheap labor, and for his pawn value in a fight against unionism.

There should be nothing remarkable or surprising in today's alliance of Negro and white workers. Its inevitability has been written, not so much in the books of America, as in the daily living of America for three hundred years. If white labor holds out its hand to black now, it is only the remote American past reasserting itself.

For the first century of our history whites were enslaved under conditions as severe as those of Negro slaves. The *Documentary History of American Industrial Society* tells us that the conditions of white indentured servants were worse than those of black slaves. "Negroes being a property for life, the death of slaves, in the prime of youth or strength, is a material loss to the proprietor; they are, therefore, almost in every instance, under more comfortable circumstances than the miserable Europeans, over whom the rigid planter exercises an inflexible severity. They are strained to their utmost to perform their allotted labor. . . . They groan beneath a worse than Egyptian bondage."

Thereafter the conditions of Negro slavery became the worst in the annals of history, and the intense exploitation of white servants relaxed, but it is noteworthy that in the early colonial period labor was labor to the operators of plantations and skin color was not significant. In this first century of Negro and white servitude, there were bonds of fraternity and association between both groups. This was to be destroyed later, as the Negro mass became chattelized. It is only now that a rediscovery of a common tradition is being made among Negro and white through the labor movement. Events and history are knocking down the fences erected between these two labor forces during the last two hundred years. The common denominator—toil—that meant something to Negro and white labor in the time of colonial plantations means something again. There can be no alternative to this because there can be no progress for either white or black alone.

It has been said, "White labor cannot be free while labor with a black skin is branded." It was this truism that compelled organized

BLACK AND WHITE LABOR

labor in the pre-Civil War period to throw its strength into the abolition of chattel slavery as a precondition for building a great trade union movement. White labor had to elevate the black man to a wage-earning status equal to its own before it could lift itself. So long as slave labor competed with white labor the slaveholders of the South and the capitalists of the North could keep the white workers' wages down, pitting one group against the other.

After the Civil War, trade unions grew all over America. But there were powerful threats to the rise of white labor and the liberation of the Negro. When white supremacy overthrew the Reconstruction legislatures, it set back and slowed up free labor in the South for a long time thereafter. It prevented free labor from getting a secure foothold in the Southern states, and it evolved a warped plantation system, half-free and half-slave, to succeed chattel plantations. Peonage, sharecropping, unemployment dogged the South from 1876 through 1930 before the most advanced thinking in white labor once again realized it could not be free while black labor remained almost as competitive a force as in 1840. Not only did a special wage differential apply to white Southern workers, but still another wage differential applied to the Negro worker on grounds of "race."

American capital has applied the "divide and rule" theory at home in as masterly a fashion as Great Britain has used it in her colonies. The employing classes from earliest times until today have found in the Negro a perfect instrument for delaying the progress of white employees. They have used the Negro as a slave, a peon, and have applied secondary wage levels for him. They have used him as a strikebreaker against whites. They have bribed his leadership, jailed his militants, used force as the final arbiter of all issues. What the modern labor movement achieves, when it asks the same pay for Negro as for white for the same work, is to strike at the heart of the "divide and rule" practice. This begins the ending of the process of using the Negro as a special fount of profits. The so-called Negro question in America cannot be solved until the same wage levels apply equally to all regardless of color. Even that is only a first step, but it is first.

That was the meaning inherent in my experience in Washington Market, and that is the meaning inherent in the common organization today of white and Negro in labor's great instruments of progress.

Today a million Negroes are organized into the ranks of labor. These may be the most significant of the thirteen million Negroes. I am sure that they lead the others. I know that the direction which Negro labor takes is the direction which the mass of the Negroes will follow. In the Congress of Industrial Organizations, in the other labor organizations, in the political parties of labor, the Negro is now a determining voice. The Negro has the problem of ending his traditional status as a specially exploited individual providing larger profits to business than white labor. Labor, in fighting for equal pay for equal work, is striking at the traditional specially profitable character of our national use of the Negro's productivity.

CHAPTER FOUR

THE GREAT MIGRATION

ONE day when I was in downtown Manhattan I saw a young Negro come out of a subway exit and look about in confusion and uncertainty. His dress and behavior attracted my notice and I stopped sharply. Where had I seen this before? He was dressed in wrinkled overalls that hung two or three inches above his ankles. He wore a tattered sweater and a banged-in straw hat. On his shoulder rested a long stick, perhaps a broom handle, and at the end of it was a reticule containing his meager belongings. He glanced about at the sight of a busy New York intersection, and there was partial fright, partial eagerness in his mien, and an obvious need for direction and help.

He became aware of my interested gaze, seemed upset by it, and started to walk off. Then I knew where I had seen him before. I had seen him in half a dozen early American newspapers and history books of the Negro. He was the runaway slave drawn by artists of the 1800's, whose picture, when published in newspapers of that period or subsequently in history books, bore the caption, "The Dash for Liberty," or "$1000 Reward for His Capture."

The temptation to find out if he was a newly arrived migrant from the Deep South was irresistible, and I smilingly approached him, holding out a dollar bill, and saying, "Did you just get in? Can I help you?"

He hesitated; I reassured him and pressed the bill upon him; and then he beamed a smile of confidence. In speech heavy with the Deep South he said he was from lower Louisiana.

"How did you get here?"

He replied that he had come part way by bus, he had walked, he had hitched a couple rides, he had been on the move for more than three weeks.

"You have relatives here?" I asked.

"No relatives," he answered, "but friends from my town if I can find them."

He asked me to direct him to Harlem, which I did. I also gave him the address of the National Urban League, in the event he could not locate his friends, so that he might secure help in finding work.

It was a fleeting, curious contact with an integral part of American history, a touching upon one of the significant processes of contemporary Negro American life: the Great Migration.

History has an inexorable continuity. Back in 1863 an abolitionist journalist, Franklin B. Sanborn, wrote an article in the Boston *Commonwealth* which contained a comment as appropriate for the present hour as it was then: "It was said long ago that the true romance of America was not in the fortunes of the Indian, where Cooper sought it, nor in the New England character, where Judd found it, nor in the social contrasts of Virginia planters, as Thackeray imagined, but in the story of the fugitive slaves."

The escape of "fugitive slaves" from the South today is a reality that may be as dramatic as the slave-time escapes of chattel. True, the Negroes who leave the South now are not always chained to plantations; it is difficult for the law to restrain them once they decide to go, and *if they have the means,* but there is a constant process of flight from the dictatorship of supremacy. It is a dramatic story, dramatic for each individual who goes North, and dramatic as a mass movement. Three or four millions of Negroes have found their way northward during the whole of American history, most of them in our own lifetime.

Their story is being told now by various writers and historians. *They Seek a City* and *Black Metropolis* recount this process. Richard Wright's *Black Boy* is a story of the migration, of his own migration, and therefore the story of many Negroes. Sociological studies of the Negro always bring in the influence of the migration and its impact on the "black metropolis" concentrations in the big Northern cities.

Some flights from the South have not been particularly dramatic, but even they are as meaningful as those "escapes" which have been made under peril. In recent years many Negroes who secured sufficient money to go, simply got aboard trains and came northward overnight. Others have had to struggle their way to the big centers of the North, and some have spent years in the process.

A city like Detroit now has about eighty-five or ninety per cent migrant Negro population. The state of New Jersey, which incidentally is almost as segregated as many Southern states, has thousands of the newly arrived. Perhaps seventy-five per cent of the Negroes in the metropolitan area in and around New York come from the South or other parts of the North. Small cities of the North often have sprinklings of recent arrivals.

Stories are told and are true of hundreds of Negroes herded like cattle into freight trains and rushed north to enter factories. Ask any Negro who came from the South how he got here and you will hear an interesting story, perhaps a dramatic one.

The South knows and has always known that its life has been based upon the Negro, upon the black man's labor, his market, even his cultural contribution. Therefore it has resisted northward movements of the Negro. The white South constantly debates this issue. A demagogic Theodore Bilbo may yell, "Send them back to Africa," but he doesn't mean it, for if he did the white primary class that has set him up as senator would have to go to work on the soil itself, and the supremacists would rather die than do that.

41]

The South lynches as an "object lesson," but it usually calls a halt at wholesale massacre, because that would be cutting off its own livelihood, its labor reserve, its very reason for being.

After World War I the Chicago *Defender* played a great part in the migration. The *Defender,* under its founder, Robert S. Abbott, a kind of Moses of the migration, urged Negroes to abandon the South and settle in the big Northern cities. The campaign to get Negroes out of Dixie was at its height. The newspaper even published timetables of train schedules out of the South. It helped set up apparatus in Chicago to receive and find employment for the migrants. The *Defender* was barred in many parts of the South. Negroes read it by lamplight in attics at night, gathering around in groups to hear of the big exodus and what their kinsmen were doing in the North. Such scenes during the present generation have been fully as meaningful as were similar covert gatherings of resisting, revolting, or departing plantation hands in the slave period.

Inevitably the authorities of Southern cities and states placed stumbling blocks in the way of Negro transit out of the South. They often refused to sell Negroes train tickets to the North; they made them declare where they were going and why; they threatened and coerced. Negroes traveled by night in automobiles that made trips back and forth between Chicago and the Southern states. They went on foot, by horse and buggy, they hitched rides.

The migration is one of the great chapters in the life of the Negro, in the life of any people anywhere, anytime. It is one of those movements such as Hegel described in his *Philosophy of History,* a philosophy based on mass movements of peoples toward freedom. Today we may look at a population shift begun by a handful of slaves back in the eighteenth century, trace it to the great Negro march on freedom of the recent war period when manpower needs pulled thousands northward and continuing migration in the postwar period, and discern in it a chapter as significant in the life of mankind as the ancient Hebrew migration out of Egypt. A kind of national Diaspora has occurred. As a result, the leavening influence of the black man is everywhere in the land today.

The migration is as old as the institution of slavery. Predating the Revolution in its origins, the northward movement reached a high point by 1855 when Harriet Tubman and other "conductors" of the Underground Railroad charted the routes of travel to the free labor section of America. At that time the numbers moving northward were in the thousands, perhaps as many as fifty thousand.

What is happening in our generation is only an extension of what went on before the Civil War when escaped slaves, through the Underground Railroad, found their way northward. At that time they came by foot, traveled at night, slept in haylofts, went north boxed in freight cars, traveled in packs armed and led by "conductors," and put up at "stations" operated by friendly allies. If the escapes of the pre-Civil War period were *always* dramatic, those of the present period *often* are; and in both periods the object has been the same: to leave a tyranny-ridden portion of the nation for a locale somewhat less oppressive.

In the era of today, within the sight and memory of most of us, this same Underground Railroad has functioned, except that it is now, by and large, an Overground Railroad. Now escape to the North is mainly out in the open. The conspiratorial "railroad" of another day has been transformed to the real locomotive and train of today. It is the same process as of old, but in high gear.

I have watched this migration with tremendous interest. To me it is one of the most significant experiences of the modern Negro. I always ask ex-Southern Negroes, "How did you get here?" So very often their stories outmatch anything that is being written or published in America today. One of the most typical migratory experiences of all was that of Bob Cook, a Negro worker whom I met in Washington Market—.

43]

We had been organizing in Washington Market for only a short time when we admitted to our "rank-and-file" trade unionist group a young Negro of about seventeen. He was slight, strong, brown-colored, very quiet. He was barely able to write his signature; and he glanced from one to the other of us, a company of ten, most of whom were white truckdrivers and porters, with great mistrust and uncertainty.

We met weekly and Bob was a regular attendant, but he remained silent. He simply observed, listened, watched how one after another spoke, and barely greeted us hello or goodbye. That went on for about six months, and I didn't know that what he saw, whites and blacks sitting and talking over a common problem, their economic plight, went counter to everything he had known before. Whites had fought and opposed him, and he had slaved for and been hounded by whites. Why, then, should he believe?

Then suddenly, just when I thought he was getting friendlier, he dropped out of sight. All that I heard was that he had lost his job and had vanished into the depths of Harlem.

One night, six months later, Bob Cook knocked at my door. He was leaner, and his clothes had become ill fitting, as if he had walked in the rain many nights. The immaturity and the uncertainty were gone. There was a friendly demeanor and he had confident command of our meeting; it was I who had become confused. Without exactly saying, "I have come to explain why I was silent," that is exactly what he did. He did it in the form of breaking down, as it were, and telling me the story of his life. It was only after this story unfolded that I realized why he had at first been quiet, withholding, puzzled by the friendly attitude of outstretched white hands.

He had little recollection of his parents, or even of the place of his birth, except that it was somewhere in Mississippi. His memories began with his fifth or sixth year, when he was suddenly orphaned and taken in by an aunt. But that lasted only a year or so, and then, he recalled, he was working. He had a "master" for whom he ran errands and did other labor for a year or two. It was a time of peonage, for which he was fed and allowed a spot in some shanty to sleep. Then he ran away—northward!

He remembered working in a five-and-dime store about fifty miles north of his previous "home." He was only seven or eight years old, and did not know how to read or write and barely knew how to talk. He worked at this place for about two years. "All I can remember is pushing boxes over the floor, opening boxes, and carrying boxes out in the back yard." He had no friends, no relatives, no child companions, but was utterly alone in the world. He worked, for he had a will to live, and he knew only that work kept him alive. It was still peonage; for his work he could eat and have a pallet on which to sleep, "where I dreamed of boxes, always dreamed of boxes getting bigger and bigger until one day the box flew open and I ran away again. I ran *north!*"

Then for a year or two he worked on a farm—"and I ate there, I ate aplenty, and I grew. I made no money but I had a place to sleep. They were white folks and weren't mean to me, but just used me all day long and fed me good."

Once more he fled, and again *northward*. "I don't know why I went north. I just went north, that's all, whenever I could make a jump. I never told them I was leaving. I made sure. I walked at night, and I took food along. Nobody ever stopped me when I jumped north." It went on like that, year after year, job after job. Sometimes he was in white hands, sometimes Negro. But he kept jumping *northward* fifty miles at a move—until he reached Chicago. He hardly knew how he got there, or why, but apparently there was everywhere a current, a process, a movement, a river, or what you will, and it said, "Go north, young man, go north."

He was fourteen when he arrived in Chicago, and still he was making his own way, finding work, having days of hunger, still without any close associations, still kinless, and knowing only work—hard, hard work. He was confused by it all, wondered why

45]

he lived on, where he was headed, looked with perplexity on the contrasts of a dominating white and dominated black world. He was tortured with a few such elementary reactions—and always the quest for food.

He lived and worked on the South Side of Chicago. Someone taught him how to write his name. He didn't know how to read but avidly watched others reading. They kept talking about Harlem, and by now the migration was in his soul; hopping a freight, he made the trip eastward.

When he reached Harlem he was directed to Washington Market where he might find work. He landed a job in the basement of one of the produce houses, sorting out and cleaning vegetables. He was strong, young, able, and willing to work for twelve dollars a week. It was grinding, heavy labor, involving again the lifting of boxes and standing in a basement whose floor was five or six inches deep with water. There he cleaned fruit and vegetables—still making things better for white people and still living in a literal and figurative world of night, when that great American social process, the labor movement, reached out its hand, tapped him on the shoulder, started him on a new road. . . .

That night he told me that after he had quit the market he had gone on relief, entered a WPA school where he learned to read and write, then joined an unemployment council where he helped secure relief for others. For months he fraternized with white labor at social affairs and political rallies. Something had clicked in his vision, and he had learned that it was true, what I and others had told him, that black and white could get together, that they had something in common—a need for sustenance.

"When I realized that," he said, "I knew I ought to come to see you."

Then he paused a minute, and he said: "I always thought I was as good as any white person. I never believed that I wasn't. But I didn't know how to say it or what to do about it."

So Bob Cook had found human dignity and station at last. He

[46

sat opposite me—my equal—as I wished it, and we were both a little elated. He had been a piece of jetsam buffeted on the great river of migration flowing northward, hardly aware how intimately he was a part of this historic process. And I think that neither he nor I quite realized then that the most significant fact of all was that this Negro migration had merged perceptibly and powerfully with the rising white labor movement of the North.

I saw him only a few times thereafter, for he seemed to be finding a new world of his own, or creating it, in the labor movement. And because he was still a migrant, something that was quite functional with him, we eventually lost track of each other.

I tell the story of Bob Cook because it illustrates so many things: the terrible oppression of the Negro, the migration, the mergence of the migration with white labor. The tie that had been established between Cook and myself has duplicated itself countless times, becoming finally a bloc alignment of a majority of the Negro vote with a majority of labor. In that lay much of the significance of a black man's and a white man's meeting in Washington Market.

When the Negroes settled in the North they were compelled to live in concentrated ghettos. There might be fifty thousand in such a quarter in some cities, or several hundred thousand in other places; but the very system that restricted them to specific areas produced an answer by creating political blocs. The Negroes realized this; they acquired a hitherto unpossessed political strength; their leaders used their voting force to make of themselves a balance of power in many cities and many states. In the 1944 elections, the Negro vote for the late President Roosevelt was sufficiently large in enough Northern states to guarantee eighty-two electoral votes to Roosevelt. The Negro had, overwhelmingly, voted with the candidate of labor.

Then, there was a delayed result of the migration that affected the South. The shift of millions of Negroes northward compelled the South to liberalize itself somewhat, lest its entire colored

47]

population pack up and move out. Movements against the poll tax, lynching, and segregation gained impetus in many parts of the South.

Thus the migration has had a salutary effect on the national economy as a whole. And the meeting up of the migration with the white labor forces of the nation has had the effect of making the whole country conscious of its obligation to liberate a whole people.

The individual meeting of Bob Cook and myself, therefore, had a symbolical meaning. He had lived through the experience of all of those colored millions who, beginning in conditions of abject misery, human indignity, and poverty in the South, have climbed their way into a somewhat better social situation, and a supremely important political position in the North. Through Cook I saw how I, like all other Americans, was bound to the history of my country. In the South, the slave trade, slavery, Civil War, Reconstruction, counterrevolution, and migration had produced Cook's northward trek into Washington Market. In the North, free enterprise, depression, labor organization had juxtaposed me to Cook in the market. White labor struggling in the North had shaken hands with black labor escaped from the South. A coming-together of two great forces in American society had taken place.

CHAPTER FIVE

LITERARY RENAISSANCE

FEBRUARY 25th, 1935, was a sunny, windy, and not-too-cold day in New York. I know because I was out in the weather for many, many hours. If one were to look at a copy of the *Daily Mirror* picture section for the following day one would see an interesting confirmation. On that day there appeared in that newspaper and in other New York dailies a photograph of writers shown picketing the Port of New York Authority building. Underneath the picture is this caption:

> *Our Future Walt Whitmans.*—Picket parade of writers in front of the Port Authority Building caused many a raised eyebrow yesterday. Genius, it seems, can no longer be denied bread. These folks say the CWA bought the services of artists, painters, etc.—why not those of jobless writers? However, latest reports last night were that the only work in sight was for the writing of more picket placards.

It happens that I led that picket line, the first in American history wherein writers banded together to get jobs, create a writers' project, and eat regularly. I am shown at the head of that procession carrying a placard reading "Children Need Books. Writers Need A Break. We Demand Projects." (Actually the clause in the placard about needing a break really read "Writers Need Bread," but it hadn't come out clearly in the print and some *Mirror* staff artist turned the "bread" into "a break.")

I'm afraid that most of us in that line, about twenty-five writers, wore a grim look. Some of us had no hats, and those of us who had held on so that the wind wouldn't sweep them off. For hours we paraded up and down shouting our need for jobs—for writers' jobs. A couple of cops moved about nervously while we treated the neighborhood to the unheard-of sight of *writers* picketing.

I recall that there were Negro writers in the line of march, and that right behind me walked Maxwell Bodenheim, at that time something of a *cause célèbre* in literary circles for the manner in which he had repudiated the risque novels he wrote in the 'twenties and "gone over to the proletariat." There were others parading that day who have since published novels, poetry, or entered journalism. Most of us were struggling in our top-floor-rear apartments trying to get out first novels. Yet it is my thought now that this group was the hard core of the then growing group of socially conscious writers. Subsequently writers' picket lines throughout New York and other big centers of the nation became not uncommon; and thereafter writers began to lend their support to the picket lines of industry.

For six months we fought and picketed all over the town. Our delegations visited government offices; we went to Washington and raised a fuss; and we formed a Writers' Union that immediately attracted several hundred writers anxious to get into a possible Federal Writers' Project. We picketed sympathetically one night in Newark, New Jersey, where a strike was on at the Newark *Ledger;* we raised the first picket line commotion in America ever to be undertaken by a body of writers—and we won the Federal Writers' Project.

Projects were set up in most states. Thousands became employed; and with this movement, the course of contemporary American literature itself was changed. Apart from the invaluable guidebooks

[50

which these projects produced, perhaps the greatest consequence was the nourishment of a body of writers who, subsequently, would take over and determine a large part of the literary production of the present period.

In this resurgence of writing generally, Negro writers shared and among them, on the New York project, were Richard Wright, Roi Ottley, Carleton Moss, and Ralph Ellison. In Chicago, Arna Bontemps, Margaret Walker, Frank Yerby, Horace Cayton, and others were sustained by Federal Writers' Project funds.

On the West Coast John Steinbeck, federally subsidized in his bread and butter days, finally issued *The Grapes of Wrath,* which brought to a high point the proletarian movement in writing. Shortly afterward Richard Wright's *Native Son* appeared. This was a book which belonged to the labor tradition yet at the same moment opened up the door to a renaissance in writing by and about the Negro. But the Negro issue was trailing the labor question by a few years. For a long time *Native Son* was destined to stand alone. For several years, until 1943, the Negro-white situation was to remain a dubious or undesirable theme to most publishers and editors.

I know just how forbidding this theme was in most publishing houses from my own baffling contact with it.

In the mid-'thirties, searching for an answer to the "unfinished business" of Negro rights, I dipped into American history, studying especially the Negro in our national past, and, in 1938, started a biography of Harriet Tubman, Negro woman Abolitionist, who, I felt, personified and could imply and dramatize the Negro woman's position in today's society. A magnificent figure, ranking in stature with any other woman in American history she had been neglected, never adequately biographized; I sought to resurrect her memory.

For four years, until 1942, I tried vainly to place this book in New York. I bumped into the most curious arguments with editors and publishers.

One, descendant of a famous abolitionist family, wrote: "You are doing an original biography all right, almost, in fact, a freak subject." He was apparently surprised or confused at reading a straightforward interpretation of a Negro woman, projecting her, not as anything eccentric, picturesque, or unique, but as a human being.

"What?" exclaimed another editor, known for advocating eloquence in the modern novel. "A book about a Negro woman? Why are you doing that? The Negro is an esoteric theme."

When I compared Harriet Tubman's stature with that of Joan of Arc to a third editor who was unaware of who she was, he commented, "You mean a Joan of Arc *of her people.*"

I didn't mean anything of the sort and there was no deal.

One publisher, whose editor had recommended the book, was set to take it. On the eve of signing a contract he changed his mind, and when I asked him why, he candidly expressed color prejudice.

"Why haven't these people come up during the past fifty years?" he asked.

It happens that the Negro has "come up" a great deal in the last fifty or seventy-five years, since Emancipation, as most people acknowledge, but I replied to him on the level of his own argument:

"Because of you. Because of me. Because we haven't let them. And you aren't going to let them come up now!"

"Because of *me?*" he remonstrated, taking my remark very literally indeed.

"Because of *all* of us," I clarified.

He was the thirtieth publisher to decline the book, so I took another look at my rejections. No two declinations gave the same reason, but all reflected hesitation based either openly on non-understanding or indifference to the Negro theme, or fear of poor sales owing to the nature of the subject. Book publishing had forgotten that a civil war was fought largely over this issue, that the biggest sellers in American history, *Uncle Tom's Cabin* and *Gone*

With the Wind, dealt with one side or another of this controversy. Nor could they forsee then that this question was destined, before the termination of World War II, to become again the crucial domestic issue of the nation, and that in the postwar period it would cut across the labor-capital conflict like a cyclone.

When my biography was finally published, in the fall of 1943, by a Negro publishing firm in Washington, the Association for the Study of Negro Life and History, several other books on and by Negroes also appeared—and an era of silence on the Negro ended in the book field. That was the season when *George Washington Carver, New World A-Comin'* and *The Darker Brother* appeared; and by then *Strange Fruit* had found a publisher, too.

Since that season the Negro issue, a major one in nineteenth-century American writing, and the Negro writer have returned to American literature. Political events and corresponding literary developments have at last succeeded in ending the more or less conscious conspiracy of indifference, opposition, and distortion which has prevailed for many decades. Negro and white writers handling this subject with understanding are back in force—in such force that Ben Burns, executive editor of *Ebony* and the *Negro Digest,* has described the trend as a "boom market." Apart from the rush of novels and social criticism, we are witnessing in the current period the seizure of Negro historiography from the control of neo-slaveholders and its re-establishment in the hands of writers who speak as part of the truest American literary tradition, that which nourishes the democratic advance of the people.

What is occurring is a flow of Negro writing comparable to the upsurge of socially enlightening literature that brightened and finally dominated the 'thirties. It has taken the form of a rather belated but decisive reply to *Gone With the Wind.* The answer is being made, not in one book necessarily, but in a barrage of them. For the simple truth is that slavery didn't go with any wind.

Since the Hayes-Tilden agreement of 1876 when the North and

the Republican Party abandoned the Negro, Jim Crow, which, to the average Negro, is little more than a form of streamlined slavery, has had seventy years in which to erode into the American consciousness. After 1876, when the federal government began to move away from the Southern question, and "states' rights" began to be restored in the South, after the Klan had counterrevolted and the Negro was left almost alone to hoe his own path, literature began to reflect this trend away from the Negro.

In 1897 there appeared one last book that reminded the country of its crucial nineteenth-century struggle. It was a memorial to Frederick Douglass, who had died two years earlier. The book was a collection of tributes to the great Negro leader, and in saying farewell to him, the volume in a way said farewell to the tradition of the human-rights issue in that century. By 1900 the Negro theme, handled from a pro-Negro viewpoint, was totally abandoned in writing, as it was nearly completely abandoned in the political life of white Americans. The poll tax had come in; Negroes were disfranchised; and the Booker T. Washington philosophy, which militated against political activity for Negroes and helped imbed supremacist notions in white Americans, swept the country. New industrial and social forces, unleashed nationally, diverted the attention of white Americans to other spheres and interests. Where whites were vitally interested in the Negro, it was in pushing him backward, as evidenced in the development of the restrictive covenant (segregated housing) nationally; and even one wing of the progressive woman suffrage movement openly fought Negro women. Writers, editors, and publishers, so often quick to follow official directions, dropped the Negro.

From 1900 to 1910 there was no literature of consequence in the Negro's behalf. But a contrary trend asserted itself in the public-school system nationally, especially in the South. In Dixie there had been instituted the segregated system of education. National history, interpreted from a Southern, white supremacist position, flooded the Southern public-school system. What did happen in

[54

that period was the rise of a Confederate historiography, and the concurrent spread of a host of myths, lies, and misconceptions about the Negro. We are still living with those untruths. There was no one book written and introduced in the school system at that time, but a great many. The *Mein Kampf* of the caste system is a whole library of books to this day distorting the teaching of the schools of the South and influencing a great many of the books used in the North. Although this "textbook question" is actually another issue, it is vitally connected with the whole matter of publishing and "literature" as it concerns the Negro.

When, about thirty years ago, the Negro American had again become insufferably isolated from the mainstream of national progress, the Negro people themselves struck back. Most of the white and Negro abolitionists had passed away. A few remaining friends of the Negro called for the reorganization of new antislavery societies to take up the unfinished tasks of the Reconstruction. Two organizations in particular sprang up: the National Association for the Advancement of Colored People, and the Association for the Study of Negro Life and History. The latter organization directed itself toward research and reclamation of the Negro tradition, and to publishing works "not acceptable to most publishers." (This clause still stands on the catalogues of Associated Publishers, which is the publishing vehicle of the Association for the Study of Negro Life and History.)

For a generation this history society almost alone carried on as the publisher of books by and about Negroes. It remained the only active force in the field of Negro literature while the whole nation pursued its policy of freezing the black man with silence. Although all of us would do well to read some of the works which that society has issued, few whites even now know of the organization's existence.

In the 1920's there was a slight upsurge of interest in Negro writing and in literature about the Negro, but, confused and groping in nature, and not touching upon the fundamentals of the

Negro-white relationship, its only real function was to open publishing avenues to a few talented Negroes. Among the best creative writing of that period was the poetry of Langston Hughes and Countee Cullen.

Not even in the 1930's can it be said that there was a body of Negro writing, or anything like a literary movement around the Negro. The black man was mentioned prominently, however, in much of the best writing. He appeared as an element, or a factor, but rarely as the main subject. Perhaps the only exception to this was Wright's *Native Son,* appearing at the very end of the decade to extend controversy in the political field and open it up in the literary world.

But after *Gone With the Wind,* with its defense of chattel slavery, came the "straws in the wind." A few books trickled from the presses: *Native Son, Let My People Go, Drums of Morning.* They came one or two a season; they were launched experimentally; there was no hearty editorial motivation behind them, but rather a "let's see what happens" attitude.

To me the most significant incident in this creeping literary resurgence was the reissue of *The Life and Times of Frederick Douglass,* by Frederick Douglass, in 1941 by a new publishing house, Pathway Press, organized just to release this one work. The book, first printed as a short narrative in 1845, was relaunched at a rather large public meeting in the West 136th Street branch of the New York Public Library, where the famous Schomburg Collection is housed. I was on hand for that symbolical event intended to recall the anti-slavery spirit and crusade, intended to project reawakening in our own period. The gathering was timed to coincide with the one hundredth anniversary of Frederick Douglass' first appearance as an orator in Nantucket. Negro and white attended the historic session, and a grandson of the late Douglass himself came to New York from the South to speak and to knit together symbolically an earlier epoch with the present.

But the literary world hesitated to get in motion over an issue

[56

already gnawing at the country's vitals. Soon after that meeting I did an article for a literary trade journal, *Writer's Monthly*, entitled "Writing About the Negro," in which I spoke of the republication of Douglass' work and said something that still holds true: "This work, by the most outstanding Negro in our history, is a virtual primer for any writer, Negro or white, seeking to explore 'the Negro question.'" I appealed to writers everywhere to look into the whole field of the white-Negro situation. Whether the piece had any effect I have no way of knowing; but, subsequently, other events in the political arena were destined to crack the problem wide open.

The resurgence of Negro literature can be traced primarily to the rise of the labor movement, the Great Migration, and more recently to the government's wartime policy of a Jim Crow army. Nothing since chattel slavery itself had incensed the Negro American and his white allies like the armed-services segregation policy. The protest against racism in the armed forces impelled the Negro people forward to a position of exceptional political maturity, and it united them as had no other issue.

Such a state of affairs was bound to be reflected in literary production, and there followed the present "flood of democracy" in writing which views the Negro as the core of the nation's social question. The quality, the tone, and the amount of the discussion is a reminder of the anti-slavery literature that was contemporary to Frederick Douglass, William Lloyd Garrison, and Wendell Phillips in the pre-Civil War period.

Within this broad wave of pro-Negro, anti-white supremacy literature, there is a segment of writing, highly meaningful, which (discussing it in the *Defender*) I called "The Blues School of Literature." There is nothing wrong with that description of the school of realism in Negro writing, and I think soon it will not be possible to dispute the fact that the blues writers, whether they be Negro or white, will have become one of the most sig-

57]

nificant corps of writers in the country's history. The books of this school reveal a realism, a brutality and closeness to the American scene unreached by such realists as Upton Sinclair, Jack London, Theodore Dreiser, and John Steinbeck. Why is this?

It is simply that for the first time in the nation's political-literary past the true thinking and being of the Negro, the most oppressed caste in the West, is being revealed; and in the course of that revelation an extreme of social living and thinking is being exposed that has been alien to the experience and even, apparently, to the imagination of the very best of the white realists. In a manner of speaking, in the same way that the present period shows signs that the Negro bloc is bursting from its three-hundred-year-old caste bonds, so Negro writers, reflecting this caste and its bursting of bonds, are bringing into the open the story of the just grievances of the Negro people. When you've got a grievance, you've got the blues; thence the protest of the Negro bloc and, by the same token, the great grim realism of these writers "privileged" to experience a most unconscionable form of submergence.

The blues literature crept into the labor writing of the 'thirties, for it was an integral part of the socially conscious wing of literature. Richard Wright, who is the pioneer and principal exponent of this "blues school," operated almost alone in the sphere for a number of years. When Wright won the Federal Writers' Project literary award established by Harper & Brothers for his book, *Uncle Tom's Children,* it was not evident then that, in this selection, two literary trends were blended. His book was viewed as a product of the labor movement, which it was, but it was also the result of another movement in American society existing coequivalent to and connected with the labor world; an area of politics and culture known as the Negro liberation movement. Wright had inherited as well as acquired the Negro base for his writings, but it had taken the labor movement to set it free, and to set him free. When, a few years later, he published *Native Son,* the character of these coexistent literary movements, the proletarian

[58

and blues schools, was re-emphasized. Actually the blues writing is an integral aspect of and deepening of the labor literature of the 'thirties.

The proponents of blues writing have operated mainly on the basis of showing the negative in Negro life, with a view to reaching the positive conclusion of indicting a white supremacist society. "Compulsive violence" is the keynote of the writing. Negro characters, shown under inordinate pressure, are portrayed in situations of murder, suicide, and violence generally. "Oppress us," says this school of writing, "and we will strike back, sometimes at you, again at ourselves, and sometimes at both of us." The writers (who, under slightly altered circumstances, might themselves be capable of the violence they have their characters commit,) rid themselves of physical compulsion through their writing, and their books rather than their fists become offensive and defensive blows at the society which submerges them. That is the reason why Jack London and Theodore Dreiser never wrote anything quite like this realism, or even imagined it. If they knew it existed, they could not identify themselves with it. In a sense this school of writing is "autobiographical." Certainly it issues from the deep well of Negro living itself.

The other principal participants in blues writing to date are Ann Petry, author of *The Street,* Chester Himes, who wrote *If He Hollers Let Him Go,* and Ralph Ellison, whose "blues" short stories have appeared in many publications. A few white writers have attempted to deal with the inner, "underground" life of Negro America but without the success of those writers who have lived it. Blues writing appears prominently and frequently in a "little magazine" which, during the last couple years, has grown up as a reflex of the Negro literary renaissance. *Negro Story,* edited by Alice C. Browning (the author is an associate editor) and published in Chicago, manages to circulate ten thousand copies bi-monthly—large for a so-called little magazine—and frankly presents all of the issues of segregation and protest, the complexities

59]

of Negro-white labor relationships, intermarriage, and all matters of color, "race," caste, class, and sex. The magazine, widely read in the publishing world, has been the means of launching a number of writers and numerous books.

But blues writing is only one wing of the Negro literary renaissance. Social criticism such as *An American Dilemma,* biographies like *George Washington Carver,* labor-Negro novels such as *Mrs. Palmer's Honey,* and the debut of numerous poets, are streams feeding the new river. We can expect the current to broaden, and I should not be surprised if it becomes once more, as it was in the 1850's, dominant in American writing. I expect this literary reawakening to merge with and help produce political factors of great consequence.

It must be remembered that the Negro is the backbone of America. He is the largest single group contributor to the national wealth. The Negro man, woman, and child is also a uniquely oppressed force. The black man has always been the central "question" of American life; and even when, ostrich-like, we would not look at it, that question was still there, large, looming, waiting for the right time to compel us to look up and around. As a result, a truly representative literature of the Negro may have been crowded out for a time, but it is cropping up again, sharply, and it will grow as a literature of freedom, grasping the attention of all of us, and none of us shall be free until, as John Brown said, "this question—this Negro question—is settled right."

CHAPTER SIX

INSIDE THE WHITE PRESS

Having worked for several metropolitan New York newspapers and one major news service, I know what editorial attitudes toward the Negro can be, and are. I well recall a remark once made to me when, years ago, I was working on the night shift of one of these papers as a rewriteman. The editor, to while away early morning hours, habitually regaled me with the "do's" and "dont's" which governed his policy. "We don't like so-and-so," he would say, "so never give him a headline break"; or, "Play up such-and-such whenever you get the chance; we're making it a national issue." And then, "When you get an assault case out of Harlem, be sure to use 'mugger' in the lead."

Use "mugger" in the lead!

And here were other front office directives: Whenever a Negro is arrested use the word "Negro" after his name; when Negro organization press releases arrive in the mails throw them in the wastebasket; when Negro delegations accompanied by white friends come to the office to protest anti-Negro policies, humor them along, perhaps moderate the policy for a few weeks, but then revert to it; when news gets scarce work up a crime wave, run an editorial demanding that the police go to work and see that they're sent to Harlem and the Bedford-Stuyvesant (Negro) area of Brooklyn; bury the news of Fair Employment Practices

Committee action the best way you can; play down Negro achievement; bury on the inside interracial improvement efforts or don't use them at all.

With this "keep the Negro in his place" attitude as the perennial policy, when a political demonstration breaks out in Harlem, as it does every few years, the rewriteman automatically knows enough to start his story this way, as this recent riot story was opened in a New York daily: "The most vicious riot in the history of Harlem occurred last night and was continuing today. . . ."

That is a blueprint of the policy applied by most New York City papers. The Negro is viewed almost without exception as a criminal element, as outside the pale of white, New York civilization. The Negro is a potential bandit. He must be treated as such: he must be singled out, guarded against, often attacked, sometimes ignored, but always segregated and isolated. Let me reformulate this seemingly incredible statement on the political level: The principle that the Negro mass of the metropolitan area is *essentially a criminal element* is as organic a policy of most big-circulation papers in Manhattan as force to maintain segregation laws is a principle in the Southland.

The irony of this imagery of crime is that metropolitan journalism itself is the real perpetrator of crime, the political-philosophic crime of pressing caste consciousness into the thinking and living of the New York citizenry. Having been intimate witness to this policy, I know how blunt and unashamed it is. The "crime wave" directed at the Negro residential neighborhoods is the most conscious crime of commission of the great dailies against the Negro. The other approach, that of ignoring Negro news, or angling it poorly, or burying it—the crime of omission—is equally significant. The fact that some few papers print news of discrimination incidents almost every day is the best evidence that the majority are following a "silent treatment" policy. Why do most newspapers handle the Negro the way they do?

I shall quote what Professor Albert Einstein said to me; I think he held the seed of it in his hand: "What is important is that there is a prejudice against people who have been misused and abused. The Negroes were brought here by greediness. And people see in them the wrong they have done to them. There is a general trend in human nature: that people hate most those to whom they have done wrong."

Let us see how the pattern works out: The notion that a "mugging" is exclusively a Negro-committed crime has been evolved especially by the Manhattan daily press. It has been developed by a few dozen managing and city editors and a few dozen police reporters who have substituted prejudices for ideas and projected angles instead of facts. Actually a mugging, as any policeman can tell you, is a special type of assault in which the victim is attacked from behind. The mugger grips his prey around the neck while, usually, an accomplice rifles the pockets. The crime has neither color nor group origin; nor is it the resort of one color more than another. There are white and black pickpockets and white and black muggers. But the press has managed, by constantly associating the term "mugger" with Harlem or with individuals specified as Negro, to whip up the notion that only Negroes engage in the tactic. This has helped foster the impression that mugging, and indeed crime, is peculiarly, or especially, a Negro characteristic. It has been built up with the same efficiency and with the same effect as the "Negroes are rapists" idea. As the rapist theme flourishes chiefly in the South, so the mugging theme has widest popularity in New York. My point in describing this is to illustrate how prejudice is fostered, how metropolitan journalism works with the racist schools of political thought.

The intermittent use of "mugging" stories is itself a preliminary to the occasional "crime wave" accounts which the newspapers resort to when headlines are scarce or when, for political reasons, it seems advisable to make an attack on Harlem.

The technique of building up a "crime wave" is a very simple one. Each night of the year scores of routine petty crimes occur in every neighborhood of the city. They are reported to local police stations and relayed to the central police office where they can be examined by police reporters. Now any time a newspaper wants to create a minor crime wave (or a major one), it has only to list all these arrests in one "roundup" story; in print, it looks like plenty of crime, and it can seem like more crime than usual if the story says it is. As a matter of fact, there is almost a murder a day in New York. Police reporters usually don't bother with them, or perhaps give them only a paragraph or two of mention. They are known as "cheap murders" because they usually occur in the poor neighborhoods where tensions and insecurity levels are high. But during a "crime wave" the "cheap murders" have their hour and get a pretty good play.

After the 1945 campaign in New York when William O'Dwyer was elected mayor, there was a temporary letdown in news developments on the European and national scenes. A "crime wave" suddenly began. It started in the offices of one newspaper, it spread to the offices of another, within one or two more editions all New York daily newspapers were infected with it except the *Post, PM,* and the *Daily Worker*. But *PM* started an exposure, and civic groups went into action demanding to be shown where there was any more crime than usual and how Negroes were any more involved than others.

During this crime wave the newspapers were featuring those roundup stories previously described. The New York *Times* even put one of its best men, Meyer Berger, on the drive, and Berger let the cat out of the bag when he happened to mention that the chief concentration of police was in Harlem where they were looking for "so-called muggers." One other thing had happened to make this crime wave important. A new police commissioner, Arthur Wallander, had come into office, and apparently the big journals felt it important to win him to their anti-Harlem, anti-Negro position at once. They combined the crime wave stories

[64

with editorials demanding action; Wallander instantly responded, and ordered special squads into the Negro neighborhoods.

In campaigns of this sort scores of Negroes are rounded up, only to be released a few hours after their arrest. Harlem becomes terrorized, and in white sectors of the community the people freeze up toward every Negro they see on the street, in a bus, in the subway. The police and the press succeed in creating a riotous atmosphere wherein Negroes, in elementary self-defense, are prepared to resist if attacked.

When I telephoned the executive editor of an afternoon paper, he defended the anti-Negro policy of that paper very openly, disdained to even deny bias, and, for example, made the comment, "What do you want us to do when they go around raping white women?"

"What rapes?" I asked.

He asked if I didn't know that a Negro had raped a white woman in a certain part of the town. I didn't know about it, but I asked whether, even if it were true, a concentration of a hundred police should be sent to Harlem.

Undisturbed when I pointed out that Albert Deutsch in *PM* had exposed the complete corruption of this particular crime wave, the editor said, "We are not interested in a racial circulation. *PM is* interested in a racial circulation."

We discussed the paper's policy of identifying Negroes where crime stories were involved. This policy, too, which is pursued day after day in the New York press, is also a preparatory educational process to the occasional crime wave. The editor insisted it was important to indicate the ethnic origin of the alleged criminal, and the only way to do it when a Negro was involved was to use the word itself after the accused's name. He was unimpressed when I pointed out this wasn't done for any other national group in the country, and he said there would be no change in that policy. The only thing he would admit was that the term "mugger" had grown to have a strictly Harlem and Negro connotation,

65]

and he said, "We're trying to get our reporters away from that."

He stuck to his general position, swore the crime wave was true, but became irritated when I gave him an explanation, as an ex-police reporter and rewriteman, of how his staff had built up the pseudo crime wave. A couple days later crime went off the front page of this paper, as well as the others. *But the citywide crime rate continued to be about the same as it had been during the scare.*

A few weeks later I joined with Councilman Benjamin J. Davis, Jr. and some others in a delegation to Police Commissioner Wallander. We brought to his attention a situation quite opposite from that reported by the metropolitan press: nine cases of police brutality in Harlem in a period of three months. With us was Mrs. Wilbert Cohen, Negro mother of a fourteen-year-old boy, innocent of any crime whatsoever, who had been killed by a policeman. The policeman was completely exonerated and transferred elsewhere.

The Cohen boy's case was "reinvestigated" and whitewashed, and remained for a time a considerable Harlem civil liberties case, until it was superseded by the police shooting of returned Negro GI's in Long Island. I gave Wallander a description of how a newspaperman writes a crime-wave story, and showed how he had leaped to obey the press. Wallander was silent.

For years the Negro press has railed against such policies of the metropolitan press, regularly carrying editorials about the practice of specifying Negro identity in crime stories. Delegations have visited most of the New York newspapers and lodged protests. During the summer of 1946 the issue came to some sort of crisis. A Long Island woman, Mrs. Marjory Church Logan, was murdered and police were looking for a suspected Negro slayer. The New York *Sun* carried a story saying that one Negro suspect was brought in for this reason: "The detective said Phillips had a funny look in his eyes and carried his head at an odd angle." Phillips, guilty of nothing, was released in a few hours. But what happened reveals how suspicion falls on all Negroes when such a broad "clue"

[66

as color is specified. Pressure from Negro groups fell so heavily on the daily press during this case, and the press made such a mess of its job that the *Times* came up with an editorial which, at first sight, might have seemed like a recantation of its policy. The *Times* belabored "extending Jim Crowism to the printed page," thus admitting that it *was* a practice of the New York press. The editorial, confirming what I have alleged in this chapter, and acknowledging the *Times's* own struggle for a Negro policy, said further: "[In crime stories] Negroes are often identified, whereas members of other races are not. This may seem a small thing. The Negroes do not think so. . . . This consideration has led us to adhere to the rule that the race of a person suspected or accused of crime shall not be published unless there is a legitimate purpose to be served thereby. By this we mean that it is correct to refer to race when the accused is still at large and race seems one mark of identification." This editorial revealed that the *Times* was under pressure, that it was being forced to reconsider its approach, that its approach hadn't been satisfactory to democratic thinking.

This policy was confirmed only a few weeks after that editorial. In a top-of-page-one story the *Times* came to the defense of Police Commissioner Arthur Wallander, who had denied that his police were guilty of brutality against Negroes. The article moved Walter White, secretary of the National Association for the Advancement of Colored People, to note in his *Defender* column that "one of the most notorious offenders in playing up crime or alleged crime by Negroes" was the *Times*. He declared that the effect of the *Times's* treatment of the Wallander story was that "the Commissioner had exculpated the Police Department, and inferentially, the *Times's* treatment of such news items." White also noted that delegation after delegation had protested the policy of the *Times* "with some improvement."

Later, discussing this issue at a Methodist forum in Harlem with James R. Wiggins, assistant to the publisher of the *Times*, Wiggins reasserted his paper's position and read the editorial I speak of.

67]

He seemed surprised at the hullabaloo from the floor, after which the meeting was peremptorily closed.

The essence of metropolitan daily policy on the Negro is to be found in the word "handling." While the *Times* leaped to the top of page one to exculpate the police commissioner, it buried on an inside page only a few weeks before the historic news that 1000 Negro and white leaders gathered in Detroit had appealed the oppressed condition of thirteen million Negroes to the United Nations Security Council.

If I had ever had any uncertainty about the position of a New York afternoon daily on the Negro, I got it directly out of the mouth of an editor of this New York newspaper. I was on the staff of *PM* when I was assigned to a press conference and luncheon on postwar housing. Looking forward to some free chicken and not much else I walked into the meeting and noticed an array of civic notables, reporters, and prosperous-looking realtors; also the above mentioned editor.

During the course of a report on the great wonders that would be performed in the way of housing after the war, I arose to ask whether the new housing would restrict the residential areas of Negroes. Would it be integrated housing for all Americans or would it extend the caste lines? I am afraid my questions at once spoiled everybody's broth.

The newspaperman boldly arose to fire the guns for white superiority and segregation for Negroes. About twenty-five citizens, many of them well known, and including Councilman Stanley Isaacs, who I remember sat opposite me, witnessed this outburst. This editor said, in brief, that segregated housing was right and necessary, that individuals had the right to decide whom they would live next to. He denounced the suggestion of integrated housing as radical agitation.

Soon after I joined the staff of *PM*, where it was understood I was equipped to handle news of Negro-white relations, I made

[68

a disappointing discovery. The editors were very reluctant to use me on this subject, even though they had announced me as a specialist in the field, and the reason was that they were reluctant and uncertain about the issue itself. I was surprised to learn that *PM* did not subscribe to a single Negro newspaper, and that they had to send a copyboy to Harlem to get one of the weeklies whenever they wanted to find out what was going on or confirm something they had heard.

I had a basic disagreement with one of the executives only a few weeks after I was with the liberal journal, on the second Negro story I handled. I was dispatched to learn whether discrimination had been practiced against a certain Harlem Democrat seeking a job as a supreme court clerk. I investigated thoroughly and found and proved that he had been discriminated against, as he had charged, but the story wasn't used because the *PM* executive didn't like the wing of Tammany Hall with which the politician was associated. In chasing down discrimination incidents it had been my experience and belief that the question of discrimination usually transcended the importance of a man's political or religious faith, and the act of exposing the bias resulted in a step forward for everybody. I was unable to convey this thought, however, and from then on I rated with some of the policy-makers on *PM* as a kind of irritation and potential bad boy.

The disciplined control over the question was revealed to me finally when I was shifted over to the Sunday department where the editor, well known for his honesty and liberalism, told me: "Conrad, you are not objective about the Negro question, so we are not going to give you any assignments in that field. We are objective and a little dispassionate in this department, so I don't feel we can trust you, with your partiality, to do an objective job."

He had used the word "objective" three times. It was a pleasure to discover, after twenty or more years of searching in the realm of social experience and philosophy for true objectivity, that it resided at last in the "Local Items" department of *PM*.

But *PM,* at least, groped toward this fundamental American problem, and it has done a good job repeatedly on specific issues. Somewhat later I found that Marshall Field, owner of the publication, was clearer on this aspect of the democratic question than many members of the staff. He told me that "Perhaps after the peace the most pressing problem in this country is the Negro question. It is almost the Number One issue. . . . All you have to do is look about you to see how vital it is."

After I had left a job on the *Journal-American,* and before going to *PM,* I sandwiched in a brief rest cure at *Scholastic,* a weekly news magazine circulating several hundred thousands to the nation's high-school system where it is used in current events and history classes. At *Scholastic* I found an attitude of nice liberality toward Negro relations, but manifesting itself chiefly in a position of caution, respect, and unwillingness to tangle with the business. Once I said to the editor, whose assistant I was, that it was time the word and the concept "race" were challenged. I suggested that it wasn't a good word to employ in describing Negro Americans. The word is divisive; it is, at best, a term used by scientists to enable them to view conceptually the large masses of people, for anthropologists agree that there is but one "race," the human race. Yet the man in the street meantime builds walls around the word, and group understanding reaches an impasse which the semantics of a scientific term alone helps to erect.

I suggested that since *Scholastic* went out as an instrument of education to millions of students, since "race" had an uncertain conceptual value, perhaps in the interest of extending ethnic democracy to ever wider areas we should use such terms as "Negro people," "Negro group," and "Negro Americans."

"I don't agree with you at all," said the editor. "The word 'race' is a very convenient term."

And that was that.

The final test of the democracy of any newspaper institution is

[70

not in the lip service which such a journal may pay the issue of justice for the Negro or any oppressed group, but in the employment policy which it follows. If a newspaper or any other organization insists that it is unbiased, one can usually check the truth of this by finding out whether or not it has Negro employees. This is particularly so among newspapers because there are hundreds of trained people now working on Negro weeklies, many of whom are perfectly capable of handling the editorial tasks of white-managed newspapers. I know this because, having worked with both, I have found that the techniques are the same. Copyreading, newswriting, even selling a newspaper, are similar for Negro and white journalism.

This test of democracy the great dailies of big, liberal New York fail. In 1946 there were no more than a half-dozen Negro reporters working on the dailies of all the New York boroughs. These papers, with a single editorial employee, operate with the proud slogan: "We are unprejudiced; we employ *a* Negro." In a way, even the employment of one is a beginning, but a beginning based usually on *not* employing others. It is a covering action, a face-saver, and an admission of an erring policy.

Writing about "Exploring Jobs in the News Field" in *Opportunity,* the organ of the National Urban League, I explained why Negroes have not been welcomed. "Newspapers are political organs," I said. "They are officially or unofficially the mediums of expression of political viewpoints. Since America is dominated by a caste system, since newspapers reflect this system more often than they fight it, since 'line' is more carefully understood and drawn in political spheres than it is in cultural environments, newspapers hold more rigidly to the traditional barriers."

In the book-publishing field the way has been opened to a great many Negro writers and to literature about the Negro; the theatre is fairly wide open to Negro talent; the world of radio has been quite receptive, although radio, like moving pictures, has been guilty of projecting dangerous stereotypes; dancers, artists, singers,

71]

writers, and others have, to some extent, been admitted to the framework of cultural production. The political parties of the left and labor have generally welcomed Negroes; trade unions frequently have Negroes in key positions of leadership; but the newspaper world remains hostile, cold, unwelcoming.

When I left *PM* and went over to the *Defender, Time* carried an account of the move in which I was quoted as saying: "No white paper is prepared to speak out on the Negro question. . . . There has been a conspiracy of silence. This is changing rapidly now, but I am apparently ahead of the trend."

What I said was true then and there has been no appreciable change in the nation's journalism since. *PM's* Negro policy has assumed more definiteness since the return from the Army of Ralph Ingersoll; the *Post* gets its occasional "exclusives"; the *Worker* has resumed pressing this issue in a manner comparable to its forceful position in the 'thirties. Around through the country there is an occasional isolated paper with a "fair-minded" policy. A few Southern papers approach the question with caution and respect. The rest is silence.

The crusading spirit, which this issue badly needs, is rare. Those wishing to express themselves authoritatively and frankly have to turn to the limited interracial press, the Negro and labor press, or to book publishers. It can be safely said that the true tradition of "freedom of the press" is no longer in the hands of the American Newspaper Publishers Association, if it ever was, but to a much greater extent in the book-publishing industry.

Call it suppression, or censorship, or indifference, or neglect, or plain dumb ignorance, and I believe it is a little of each of these, the point is: the great non-military civil war in our own midst goes almost wholly unreported by the white press. Not even George Seldes' alert little "conscience of the press," *In Fact,* has yet developed initiative enough to examine the weekly Negro press and to report what the white press won't print. In fear and trembling

[72

the press looks to its duties with too little too late, just as the public officials, the legislators, the school boards, and the major political parties have come through too late with the same too little.

In fact, journalism in New York, and in the large centers of the North, and in a great majority of Southern centers may be considered the last strong bulwark of the caste system itself, short of the Southern officialdom and its copperhead allies in the federal and Northern state governments.

The daily newspaper is one of the greatest instruments for making up the people's mind. The press, if it took up the Negro issue properly, could help alter the practice of the nation. But the American Newspaper Publishers Association has seen fit, in the main, to perform oppositely. It is either actively anti-Negro or it is silent. Either course is an attack on one-tenth of the nation. It is also, in the long run, an attack on the other nine-tenths.

CHAPTER SEVEN

THE NEGRO PRESS

"RIGHTEOUSNESS Exalteth a Nation."

No, I am preaching no sermon. That quotation appeared on the masthead of the first Negro newspaper, issued one hundred and twenty years ago. Published in New York, *Freedom's Journal* was the creation of two abolitionists, the Reverend Samuel E. Cornish and John B. Russwurm. It was a small-sized periodical, and the type face was small, but the columns were packed with a religious wrath. The newspaper very probably influenced William Lloyd Garrison, the white crusader who, six years later, launched his historic *Liberator* and opened the epoch of the moral anti-slavery campaign.

Freedom's Journal was intended for Negro and white readers, but perhaps chiefly white readers, for the number of Negroes who then could read was probably not very great, and the power to liberate the Negro lay principally in the hands of whites. The idea was to win friends for the abolition of the use of men as property.

From about 1830 until 1860, Negro-edited and Negro-owned newspapers flourished. To mention only a few, there were the *National Anti-Slavery Standard,* issued in New York; the *Anglo-African,* a kind of intellectual "quality magazine" also published in New York; *Frederick Douglass' Monthly,* printed in Rochester; and the *Principia,* published in Philadelphia and having a strong

Quaker tone. As the abolitionist crusade strengthened and spread, many daily and weekly newspapers, white-operated, picked up a strong anti-slavery character, and philosophically trailed the Negro press.

The Negro press then can be compared in function to the political leaflet of today. Its purpose was to inform, arouse, and mobilize. It was the spiritual ancestor, not only of the essentially agitational Negro press of this day, but possibly of the modern labor and radical press.

In the early days of this journalism it was not at all a community press and it never existed for the Negro group alone, in contrast with the way many Negro-owned papers of today operate. Its character was almost totally political, and even revolutionary.

But something happened after the Civil War. As a consequence of the federal government's abandoning its protection of the Negro in the South after the election of Rutherford Hayes to the presidency, leaving the black man to the mercy of Southern rule, the caste system was swiftly brought into existence. State and local decrees compelled Negroes to live in segregated parts of Dixie's cities. Concentrations of Negroes occurred in the larger urban areas; cities like Atlanta and Birmingham developed special quarters where Negroes were massed. Thousands marched northward to continue living in segregated areas of cities like Chicago, Detroit, Philadelphia, Pittsburgh, and New York. Compelled to live apart, their group feeling deepened. The American world, North and South, became a world with little Negro "worldlets" in each community. The Negro's social existence drew inward, for it was not allowed to expand. To intensify the process, Booker T. Washington came along with his extraordinarily mistaken policy: "In all things that are purely social we can be as separate as the fingers, yet one as the hand in all things essential to mutual progress." His outlook resulted in more segregation laws all over the South, and it widely infected Negroes who drew ever deeper into the caste shell. The Negro began to build a life and culture within the framework of "colored" or "racial" group living; and a Negro press based upon a community viewpoint, and often premised on a simple and outright profit motive, sprang up.

This new press retained, as its central theme and reason for being, the need for protest. But the columns devoted to protest, to reporting incidents of discrimination or intergroup collaboration became mingled with columns of news of professional, business, and social doings.

There was no uniform pattern in this development, nor is there today. The *Defender* grew up in the crusade of northward migration. It had a period in the 1930's when it was the rankest kind of crime and scandal sheet, but it lost circulation then, and resurged around 1941 when the militant policy resumed. Responsibility for the paper as the Number One journal in the Negro field in recent years, in terms of political impact, has been exclusively the progressive editorship of Dr. Metz Lochard. The name, *Defender,* is itself revealing, for *defense* is probably the fundamental *motif* of Negro life. There is no such thing as "thinking like a Negro" or "thinking like a white"; but the Negro reasons and reacts about the white on the basis of his *defenses,* and the white man thinks about the Negro according to the degree and activity of the prejudices he holds. Probably the most constant social emotion of the Negro individual and group is that of defense against the prejudices, pressures, and economic handicaps established by the white world.

As an example of the wide diversity of ideology in the Negro press, there is the New York *Amsterdam News,* which is a ghetto-community semi-weekly. This organ frankly acknowledges that it exists for the sake of making a profit, and it only does lip service, in my estimate, to "the cause." Such a paper represents the full development of the Negro press as a business institution and a community newspaper idea. My friend, Julius Adams, its associate editor, discussing his newspaper at a conference in Harlem called to talk over the function of the Negro press, pointed out: "A newspaper is a commodity. A commodity must be served up the way it will sell." Here then is a paper which has lost sight of its origins in protest and in group defense. Modeling itself stylistically very much after the New York *Journal-American*, the *Amsterdam News* finds itself often on the unpopular side of social controversies. Twice in its history its employees have struck; its columns and pages seem totally devoid of policy; and yet, because it is loaded with social news, gossip, scandal, and advertising, it has a big circulation.

The names of these newspapers also reflect the chronic debate within the community over questions of national-ethnic-anthropological relationships. I have mentioned the early periodical, *Anglo-African*. In Baltimore there is a flourishing weekly called the *Afro-American;* there is an *Oklahoma Black Dispatch;* and a number of papers have the word "Colored" in their mastheads. Negroes are divided about what they think they ought to be called. The old color divisions such as mulatto, octoroon, and quadroon are no longer in use. These distinctions definitely and exclusively belonged to slavery, to the period when human beings were sold on a physical basis and the color gradation had a cash value. The terms in widest use today are "Negro" and "colored." They would like to be called Americans, or just people like the rest of us, and that's what the fight is all about.

I once came upon this question of what the Negro ought to be called, according to a Dixie view, when I was visiting in Alabama. A cab driver who could tell from my accent I was from the North started talking candidly to me as Northerner and Southerner. As he drove me into the Negro quarter he described what mighty fine people lived thereabouts. He once had an insurance collection route in that neighborhood and had intimate contact with the people. But he kept using the word "niggers." Then I asked: "By the way, what do you call colored people when you speak to them? I'm curious to know because you say you get along with them so well and you seem to have dealt with them."

"Oh, sure," he obliged. "I gets along with them fine. I just calls them niggers, coons, darkies, shines—whatever they likes best."

I do not intend to get afield of the question of the Negro press: in the overall nature of Negro journalism, the problem of terminology becomes easily a perspective through which to view most facets of the question.

In the main, Negro newspapers more or less correlate the several functions of being a protest organ, a profit-making institution, and a community newspaper. But if a new journal is to succeed it has to represent in some way the group's political interest. In origins the press's purpose is to advance the Negro or denounce and expose origins of white pressure. In practice, it is often a different matter. Not for a moment do I want to convey any illusory impressions about the Negro press today. Like owners of the great white dailies, the big weeklies have no fondness for the Newspaper Guild, and resist the Guild quite as strenuously as Hearst. I have no photostat copies of greenbacks that have changed hands, but I have come to the conclusion that many of the Negro newspapers will throw their election-time support to the highest bidder. I know that this belief may seem in shocking contrast to all I have said about the zealous, pro-group character of the Negro press; but it is terribly true, and I think the Negro masses need to know more about it than they do.

What is reprehensible about this practice is that the big Negro newspapers are profit-making and the top executives and owners have incomes ranging from $10,000 to $30,000 and upwards a year, and there is therefore no reason for a sellout. They are not in want as are their people. This violation of trust is not to be confused with Uncle Tom-ism. The Uncle Tom idea connotes weakness, collaboration, passivity. But the big Negro press thrives on "race militance." Therefore, when it betrays its own, the operation is comparable to quislingism. One of the best services I can perform for the Negro "average man" at the moment is to convey this truth to him. It is also a service to the Frank Sinatras and the Henrietta Buckmasters, for of what avail is it to the white fighters for Negro advancement and honest Negro leadership if their work is to be canceled out in critical election moments? This situation has implications of dynamite for the 1948 elections, because the Negro vote may be determined by the Negro press. In the current disillusion with Truman, prevalent in Negro ranks, those papers which, in 1944, sold themselves to the Republicans (while praying for a Roosevelt victory) now have a better excuse, a rationalization, for possible "deals" with them in 1948.

But the real area of danger lies in the public-relations treasury of the Republican Party, which has had great success in reaching big Negro weeklies. With the political situation so uncertain, it is important for the Negro man-in-the-street to guard against 1948 sellouts.

When I was in Georgia recently I talked with two white politicians from Arkansas who spoke to me as "one white man to another." One of them said: "We voted the colored this year for the first time. But nothin' to worry about. They voted our way. We bought out their leaders."

Also, Eugene Talmadge, the Governor-nominate of Georgia, gave me the names of two Georgia Negro leaders who voted for him. Whether for money or love, I don't know. Quislingism is the Negro's greatest internal enemy.

Finally, it is the Democratic and Republican Parties which bear the first responsibility for such "deals." They deduce it is cheaper to buy the Negro press than to pass progressive minority legislation. Also, when they pay off the Negro papers they feel that their obligation is largely taken care of and they don't have to worry; with the Negro publishers and chief editors involved in guilt the major parties can ignore much of the year-round pressure which the Negro press exerts. What this process amounts to, finally, is another form of supremacist control of the Negro group.

I once had a discussion on this point with Leslie Perry, a Washington lobbyist for the National Association for the Advancement of Colored People. We were speaking of the fact that during the 1944 presidential election several of the big weeklies turned their papers over to candidate Dewey, while the people in their communities voted overwhelmingly for Roosevelt. We mentioned the name of one publisher who cashed in on Dewey, and, it was said, prayed for a Roosevelt victory. Perry believed that this purchasability wasn't known to the Negro people; he urged I write something about it somewhere, and this is it.

What is important about the fact is that the Negro man in the street went over the heads of this type of journalistic leadership when the voting hour came.

Also it shows that Negro publishers are as human as the white publishers who operate on the same principle of profit, the only difference being that the latter are influenced chiefly in the form of advertising. The Negro press proceeds on the same economic principles as govern white journalism; human nature seems to be the same in both groups. If, in the main, the white press is conservative-reactionary, so too is the most influential Negro press.

None of this alters the fact that the overall effect, week by week, year around, of the Negro press is that of an educational and protest impact. With the exception of a few election-time sellouts, and those few papers which pander to crime and gossip, the rest are overwhelmingly Negro-group papers. Year-round protest: election-time reaction. That is the anomaly of the big Negro press.

Anyone who thinks that millions of people can read such protest week after week and not become informed is simply deluding himself. Yet there are the naive, millions of them with white skins, who actually believe that the Negro doesn't think, that he has no intelligence, and no desire for improvement. But the Negro knows just about what the white man thinks; he knows where to go to get the right information about him; and he knows exactly what his relationship is in the community to the "democratic question." The only thing he may be uncertain about is what to do about it, how to deliver himself from his situation, whom to believe in,

[80

what philosophy to take up. Even here the Negro press attempts to provide the answers.

One newspaper that has had a wildfire growth and a great influence, although not a very large circulation, is the *Michigan Chronicle,* which was started in Detroit about ten years ago by a young man named Louis E. Martin. Martin decided on a policy of lining up the Negro group with the CIO. As a result, his paper became a potent political force; and when the Detroit intergroup clashes occurred during the war some reactionary individuals blamed Martin for "provoking the riot." Actually Martin had helped weld the Negro community into a unified bloc, and he had taught them that their natural ally was the white workingman with whom they must collaborate as well as compete.

My thought is that too often the Negro press has veered over into the "community paper" approach, and that it has ceased to have an impact on the white community—which was its essential intent. As Dr. Metz Lochard of the *Defender* put it, "The Negro paper is a corrective." Its job is to correct the lopsided caste-class setup. Speaking before a group of Negro Newspaper Guildsmen in New York once, I urged the staff workers to find means of bringing their press to whites in business, labor, civic, fraternal, and religious areas. I urged them to distribute their papers free if necessary and, if they could sometimes afford to, to the officialdom locally, state-wide, and federally. This would place their criticism and protest directly in the hands of those under attack; for usually, I pointed out, those under fire in the Negro press never knew about it.

When I went over to the *Defender* and had, in the main, a Negro audience, I felt that what I was saying and doing was, in a measure, like rain falling on a lake. I was telling Negroes what they already knew, when I felt that the important thing was to reach whites who needed this knowledge. Wherever the Negro press acts on the "community paper" principle, there exists still the disastrous social philosophy of Booker T. Washington. We have to remember that the ultimate objective is to break up and end the caste system, not to perpetuate segregated communities and "community newspapers."

I sharply disagree with Mr. Gunnar Myrdal, the sociologist author of *An American Dilemma,* in his conclusions about the Negro press. He sees a continuous development of the Negro press based on its present specialized Negro-group character. He says: "Meanwhile, gradual improvements will only strengthen Negro concerted action as they will seem to prove that the Negro protest is effective. All improvements will give the Negro press more big news and important issues to discuss." He is reasoning about the press in terms of its future as a business institution. Since, he contends, also injuriously, that the Negro will not likely enjoy his full constitutional rights in this generation "and, perhaps, not in the next," the Negro press is going to have a future based on the continuance of segregation.

If Myrdal had spent more time living with the inner politics of the Negro press, he would reach other conclusions. If he could see the big papers trembling in their competition with each other at this very moment, torn between whether they should remain weeklies or become dailies, whether they should be protest or scandal papers, whether they should concentrate on more newspaper coverage or become more like magazines, more Negroid or more interracial, he would know that an hour of transformation of the Negro press is at hand. What is happening is this: Responding to the developed interracial movement, the Negro press is already considering the practicalities of becoming broadly interracial, representative of groups in addition to the Negro. The *Defender* has begun a move in this direction. If the Negro press does not move that way, white-owned papers like *PM* and the New York *Post,* and new ones to come, will spread out over the Negro community, embracing its interest in their pages and welding that interest to the political objectives of other social groupings. If the struggle for integration has any validity, that is the only thing

[82

that can happen; that is the only course this press can take as it pictures the breaking up of the caste system. Those papers which remain strictly Negroid in character will tend to hold back the movement toward integration; they will become increasingly reactionary and nationalist, will cling to caste-status outlooks.

Although it is a just complaint that not enough whites read the Negro press, it happens that many whites, especially women, do read the *Defender*. During the war I heard from many soldiers, Negro and white. Several Negro GI's wrote bitterly of their experiences and said there was "another cause" they would fight for when they got home. A Southern white lieutenant wrote that what he had seen and experienced taught him a new respect for the Negro, and that when he returned to the States he meant to lend his energies to securing justice for the people of color. White women readers, in particular, have asked what they might do to advance intergroup good will. I have heard from white women in most states of the union. They have told me of their intergroup activities and sought advice on how to work effectively. Young Negro writers and artists all over the country have sent me their products, seeking help in getting established.

What has impressed me mostly in this "fan mail" has been the interest of the white women. Their concern for the Negro has a very understandable background. In 1848, at a Women's Rights Convention in Seneca Falls, New York, a Negro, Frederick Douglass, was the first man in America to raise his voice for woman suffrage. Subsequently the suffrage and the abolitionist movements joined hands. The Negro and women's causes were united until 1868. Yet white women still had two generations to go before they could vote. Still seeking their political rights in America, white women automatically make spiritual and practical alliance with another discriminated-against group.

Is there a free press in America?
The reader will recall the description of the newspaper office of

the *Alabama Tribune,* the weekly published in Montgomery, Alabama (*v.* Chap. I). This was an office which was more or less the spokesman for the thousands of Negroes in Montgomery and for those in the vicinity of Alabama's capital city. It was such a cramped, struggling sight compared with the vision of the great forty-story building which houses the New York *Daily News,* that I could not help but juxtapose the two antithetical forces in American life: at one extreme the great daily which variously maligns or ignores the Negro, and at the other, the small tooth-and-fang weekly that fights the great Goliath of caste even while trapped like an animal in some small backroom in a faraway Southern city.

I was struck with the "underground" nature of the Negro press, certainly in that community, when, talking with a Southern white aristocratic woman who was supposed to be interested in the Recy Taylor civil liberties case, she expressed surprise to hear that there was a Negro-edited paper in the community.

"What? You say there's a Negro paper here? A weekly?"

She was astonished, incredulous, and angry.

I do not know how many Negro newspaper offices there are like that in America, but I do know that there are about two hundred and fifty Negro weeklies, and together they form something like the political vanguard of the Negro bloc. It is their task to inform the Negro people of the truth about their relations to the *Herrenvolk* (as I have heard Negroes refer to whites), and act also as political protestors against segregation.

I know that my own paper, with a great national circulation, issued in a fair-sized three-story building in Chicago, is often concerned with the question of suppression in the South. Yes, the Negro press can be and often is *suppressed* in the South. In spite of all the talk about freedom of the press, the Chicago *Defender* has repeatedly been taken off newsstands in the South. It has even been halted at post offices. And in the handling of the news, the

Defender's editors often consider whether specific banner headlines will bar the paper from the stands of certain cities.

A free press? Yes, there is a "free, white, and twenty-one" press, so to speak, but the test of whether there is full freedom of expression and representation in journalism is answered in the living editorial written by the very existence of a special Negro journalism. These newspapers have come into existence as an expression of the conscious exclusion of the Negro from the national life and, hence, from daily journalism too. This mass of Negro newspapers may be the most interesting footnote to contemporary national history: the journalism of a caste, the journalism of involuntary expatriates, the protest and community newspapers of a people exiled on their own soil!

CHAPTER EIGHT

THE RESTRICTIVE COVENANT

"The right of life, liberty and property, the Supreme Court of the United States has repeatedly held, is not a Federally secured right."
—ATTORNEY GENERAL TOM C. CLARK
in the *N.Y. Herald-Tribune*, Nov. 3, 1946.

HERE are a few impressions from the average day of a white newspaperman whose voluntary beat is Harlem. . . .

Always there is the feeling that what I am reporting is not just "news" or "correspondence" or "features." What I see and describe is usually so explosive in implication that I keep thinking of it in military terms, as if my office were an advanced position on some real fighting front, in a war now still in a kind of guerrilla stage. Actually my headquarters is in the heart of the throbbing community of New York, at the busy corner of 125th Street and Seventh Avenue. My phone jangles all day, typewriters are apt to be going most of the time, the floor is sprinkled with paper in the traditional deshabille of the newsroom, people are running in and out, like couriers, bringing the tidings of the battle outside.

I reach for a cigarette and a light. The words on the matchbox catch my eye. "Stamp out venereal disease," it says. "Be sure. See your doctor. Be examined. Have a blood test. Phone, write, or consult the Harlem Council on Social Hygiene, 2238 Fifth Ave. Films—Lectures—Literature—Exhibits."

I wonder how the matchbox got on my desk, who chanced to leave it there, then toss it aside, thinking of how the matchbox typifies the constant alertness of the community, the never-ending struggle against disease, crime, poverty, and perhaps the most galling grievance of all, *segregation*.

I open the window and the traffic noise is earsplitting. Wheels screech, horns bark, exhausts pop like machine guns, and, looking out the window, I can see the rush of black and brown faces, like soldiers, moving up and down the main street of Harlem, 125th Street. They can look up, too, and see the big black-and-white banner of the *Defender,* and perhaps they view it as a kind of gonfalon as they laboriously advance over the rough democratic battlefield that is the nation.

Down below, at this moment, I see the "grenadier." He is a lean, hungry-looking, pathetic fellow who was in World War I. He threw grenades then, and he is still throwing them. Now they are imaginary grenades, and before he tosses them, he gathers a crowd around to look on. They look on all right, for the grenadier is covered with political buttons, Willkie and Roosevelt and Hoover buttons, Labor Party and War Relief buttons, Red Cross and Chinese Aid buttons. He's covered from head to toe with them—a living symbol of the movements in society for the last decade or two. "Look out, now," he yells, "here it comes." Then he throws it, with a great flourish of his arms, and in stony silence the symbolical grenade explodes. But perhaps the projectile he throws is not imaginary. Perhaps it is prophetic. People don't laugh joyfully at the grenadier.

Along the street there approaches the large woman with the anguished eyes. She sells shopping bags. I see her daily in front of one of the markets calling out wearily, monotonously, "Buy b-a-a-g, buy b-a-a-g." And her eyes roll in a queer kind of pain. She is walking with pain, too. I don't dare talk to her. I know the tragic history of the woman without questioning her. I can see the trip North she took many years ago to escape the South's pressure. I can see the unemployment, the hundreds of washes she has laundered, the disease, and the evictions in her background.

Opposite my office rears the twelve-story Theresa Hotel. It is the only hotel in Harlem worthy of the name, but everybody puts it down as a very secondary institution indeed. It is where colored big shots put up because it's not pleasant to try to get into hotels downtown where you're apt to be softly but definitely told everything is filled up.

I glance down 125th Street, and I still get that impression of a long trench going crosstown, the buildings on either side but facades concealing gunfire. A long trench, with figurative, perhaps literal, gun emplacements along the line. Police patrols move up and down the street, crowd the people on the curbs. I see bitterness in the eyes of the Harlemites at these "storm troopers," as I've heard them called. Plainsclothesmen mingle with the crowds, noting the faces of people going in and out of organization headquarters. Colored folks are walking in and out of white-owned stores, buying things and leaving a profit. And 125th Street is the source of one more stream of psychological warfare running through the town; it is almost never without a slogan-shouting picket line.

I go out into the street to call at some organization office, and the sea of dark-tinted faces closes about me, like a rush of water, everywhere I go. Often I think of the Negro in the imagery and symbolism of rivers. I suppose many people do.

I look west on 125th Street, and I see the crosstown avenue fade into the maze of Riverside Drive buildings. I know what is going on there: Negroes, needing living space, are reaching into the apartment buildings silhouetted against the Hudson River's sky. I look south to where, only fifteen blocks below, Central Park constitutes a barrier to Negro residential penetration. I look east

[88

only a few blocks away to Lexington Avenue, where the Finnish, Puerto Rican, and Italian neighborhoods open up and there is another residential barrier based on color. Each of these distances against which Harlem tenements crush outward is a "tension area." I live in the remaining tension area, the northernmost section of Harlem, Washington Heights. Three years ago, when I moved into this neighborhood, then all white, Harlem ended about fifteen blocks below. Now Harlem has moved upward, house by house, to within a few streets of where I live— like a military column taking a town block by block.

I pass through this restricted area, a voluntary inmate of a sprawling fortress, preferring this ground on which to fight to any other, using this semi-concentration camp as a base from which to fire what missiles a newspaperman can fire. I march down the street, often thinking hotly of what I see. There may be a symbolical grenadier, or the stump of a legless woman shrieking from a street corner where she begs, or youthful independent zoot-suiters in front of a theatre or poolroom, or prostitutes and pimps who halt me; but overall there is an army of serious-purposed individuals, mostly working people, or, what is just as likely, of people looking for work. There are housewives with children at their skirts; there is the stenographer entering the stationery store; the cab driver turning the corner. There are the people buying at the stores, the same people with the same desires one finds everywhere. I see one brown-skinned man with Irish features; a redheaded Negro girl with perhaps Scotch in her parentage; here a Spanish quality in the face; there a combination of Englishman, American Indian, and Negro. For all of "white" and "red" and "yellow" America has been drained into the brown and black bodies. The ethnic diversity convinces me that the Negro, more than any other American, conveys the truest "melting pot" nature. The main ingredient of this boiling kettle of international personalities is the black man; and this that is called the "Negro" face reveals the inpouring of the world.

89]

But all this is only phenomena. All this is only the surface, and the surface of Harlem is no more Harlem than the skin of a man is the man. I know that whatever I see here is but the end-result of centuries of development, and that the true meaning of Harlem is in the processes and movements and history that underlie its existence. I know that one does not see all this by a walk through the streets, but that, like the land under the water, and the water under the sand, the true Negro must be found elsewhere than in the immediate phenomenon. To see what I have mentioned here would be only a visitor's tour by auto through the community, and this reveals nothing but that the truth is hidden.

Even so, I have mentioned the surface and shown the people moving in the streets, and suggested the tense borders of the community, for one great truth can be revealed through the externals. Not for an instant can I escape the feeling that here is a closeted community. It is like steam held tightly in bounds, yet likely to burst the rivets at any time. This is always my main awareness. The crowded streets, filled with black and brown faces, keep saying: "Out beyond it is for others. This is our world, our domain, our unwanted destiny. For us the dwelling together as a pariah caste." And it is to this segregation, sometimes called "the restrictive covenant," that I now proceed.

One evening, while I was with a group of Negro acquaintances who were discussing Jim Crow, someone mentioned that migrants from Southern states tended to band together in Harlem, to live in certain neighborhoods and maintain fraternal, even economic, ties on a basis of regional origin.

"Did you know," this observer remarked, "that on West 135th Street there's a club that calls itself the Sons of Georgia?" Some didn't know, so the same informant continued, "And over on 123rd Street there's the Sons of North Carolina Benefit Society." He paused to let that reach us, then resumed, mentioning the Sons of Florida and the Sons of South Carolina and their approximate residential areas. But at this point someone put in wearily, "Yes, I know, and around them all the Sons of Bitches."

That is about as good an illustration as I know of the Negro's desperation of being hemmed into ghettos and victimized by the restrictive covenant, or, as it is also called, "the racial covenant."

Cab drivers often harbor resentments against Harlem and they will frequently make efforts to avoid taking passengers there. Trying to find out why taxicab men sometimes hesitate or outrightly refuse to enter Harlem, I have been told that "It isn't safe," or "I know a driver who got held up there," or "They don't tip."

That some drivers have had unfortunate experiences in Harlem is doubtless fully as true as that cabbies have had things happen to them all over New York, but it is my belief that Harlem has become a Frankensteinian rumor that circulates among white drivers in "the barns." The fear of entering Harlem matured after the riot of August, 1943. But this was no demonstration against white individuals. No individuals were hurt. It was protest against the wartime policy of a segregated Army, against unemployment, against the segregation of the blood of white donors from that of Negro donors, against the restricted residential areas, against non-employment of Negroes in many white-owned stores of Harlem, and against the whole system of Jim Crow. But individuals are no more insecure in Harlem than anywhere else in New York. I found out how unreasoning this fear is from the *diverse* answers given by cab drivers. They themselves did not know why they really wanted to avoid the community. If they really knew each would have had the same answer. But they ran the whole gamut of the answers of bigotry.

"Dey ain't so smart," said one barely literate cabbie to me. "I like to have smart customers wit me so I can talk wit dem."

Once, a driver gave me a curious look and told me to hop in. He started his car, went a few blocks, then simply put the brakes on and halted. "Sorry, my car has broken down," he explained. But it was only his nerve that had broken down.

Another declined going to Harlem by saying, "Not me, brother. I don't go up there, not for a million bucks. I don't want any trouble."

"Have you ever had any trouble there?"

"I've never had any because I've never gone there." There was the perfect reply of the individual terrorized by rumor, prejudice, myth.

Finally, it is the physical fact of Harlem's specialized location that frightens drivers away. It is a shock to the emotional system to pass directly from all-white areas into all-black neighborhoods. Society intends that shock. Government protects it. Men of all colors suffer from it. You get close to the base of it when you get into the question of property. . . .

A landlord in midtown New York, where I once lived, said to me: "You'll have to leave. I don't want Negroes to come into my building, unless they come up the service elevator. I don't mind myself, but your neighbors have been complaining." To make a deal he offered me the place rent-free for the remainder of the month and for the following month. "Now I don't want any trouble," he added, "and I think I've made a fair offer." I answered that I preferred the trouble. "All right, you'll get it," he assured me. For the remainder of the term of my lease the landlord was unpleasant, denied service to the apartment, and it was important that he got his rent on the very date due.

How the New York City government protects this separation of the two groups is illustrated in the experience of an acquaintance, Robert McAlpin, a light-colored Negro, who was standing on a street corner in Harlem late one night when plainclothesmen picked him up and asked to know what he, a white man, was doing in Harlem after midnight. McAlpin, a photographer on a Harlem newspaper, saw an opportunity to teach the police that there is no longer any certainty about just who is white and who is Negro. He let them take him to the police station. When he

[92

revealed and proved he rated as a Negro by American law, the police let him go.

There was no legal base for arresting him whether he was white or Negro. The story broke prominently in the Negro press. The implication in the arrest was that white men should keep out of Harlem. Its meaning was that police were trying to enforce Southern segregation law in the biggest liberal city in the country even when there was no law to validate the police action. It is a logical extension of the policy of unquiet desperation which marks the pattern of suppression employed wherever there is illiberal government.

One of the best illustrations within my own experience, placing the responsibility for the restrictive covenant right where it belongs—with realty interests—occurred in August, 1944, when I was on *PM* and when I was assigned to investigate a discrimination charge brought by Madame Grete Stueckgold who, for a long time, was a Metropolitan Opera prima donna. She was living in a penthouse on the upper East Side when she received a notice from her landlord, saying that she was not welcome to renew her lease and must get out. The singer, who was giving vocal lessons, had taken on about ten promising Negro pupils during that year. She suspected the reason for the arbitrary order but needed confirmation.

I started checking and had unusual luck. One woman admitted the management had asked her if she objected to her neighbor's Negro callers. The superintendent blandly confessed he had kept track of the number of colored people making daily calls at her penthouse. An Office of Price Administration spokesman bluntly said, "What is at the base of this situation is the color question." Everybody talked to me as if I had hypnotized them, including finally the vice-president of the realty firm who, though he wouldn't confirm or deny Madame Stueckgold's accusation, admitted that if Negroes sought tenancy in the building, "We would probably find some gracious way of not admitting the tenant."

Deep are the roots of segregation.

The restrictive covenant, a legal term of which even many lawyers do not know the meaning, is responsible possibly more than any other one feature of our society for non-understanding between Negro and white, for the fortress of myths, suspicions, rumors, and hatreds that abound within the two groups.

The classic summary of this was made by Premier Jan Christian Smuts of the Union of South Africa when he was in this country. Asked about the status of Negroes in his dominion, Smuts answered: "We have no Negro question in South Africa. We have segregated the living districts of the Negro and the white. Once you settle the matter of where each lives everything else flows from that. Separate the blacks from the whites and everything is automatically under control; everything else takes care of itself in logical sequence."

What Smuts said and meant was simply that the minute society separates people from each other by color and class, it sets in motion diverse economic, psychological, and cultural processes. Society builds two antithetical cultures side by side. They can be different economies and different cultures separated by a railroad track, or a picket fence, and one can then pit one culture against the other and make each group hate and misunderstand the other, while at the same time guaranteeing a continuance of profits for the class at the top of the two-layer cake.

Now when such adjoined peoples do not mingle, do not integrate, each group is compelled to fall back upon imagination and secondhand information for knowledge of the other. Meantime that group responsible for the segregation—in our time elements in the Anglo-Teutonic segment of society—has fostered one fundamental philosophic idea: that the Anglo-Teutonic type is organically, inherently, naturally, and even by divine right superior, while the segregated man is so treated because organically, inherently, naturally, and even by divine designation he is inferior.

[94

It is no accident that Smuts, for Britain, has summed up the policy so well. Smuts stated the great historic pattern of "divide and rule" very simply. The British have always been the masters of this policy. They introduced it to America, and they introduced it in South Africa, and, indeed, wherever they could throughout the world. The British, lords of the slave trade, picked up their cargoes of black ivory, transplanted them to the West Indies and American plantations, and planked them down on the plantations into ready and waiting cradles of segregation evolved by British colonial slaveholders.

In fact, so ingrained is the idea of "nationalism," of "race," and of ethnic difference generally in the British mind that once a British subject, J. King Gordon, the Canadian managing editor of the liberal *Nation,* referred to the French and the English as different *races*. I asked him why he used the word "race" to describe English-Canadians and French-Canadians. He explained that it was the English (his own ancestors) who used *race,* but that the French-Canadians were more likely to refer to the English as *les Anglais.*

I cite the British perfectionism only because I want to suggest the antiquity of color prejudice inculcated for economic purposes and to indicate that modern American origins of Jim Crow stem specifically from the royal British regimes engaged in slave trade in the seventeenth and eighteenth centuries, and from the British-born colonial planters. The British deposited caste upon our shores. They still practice it with even finer precision in South Africa than we in Atlanta or Manhattan. But after the British flood, came the American deluge. . . .

Back in the days of chattel slavery, it was not necessary to have laws on the books restricting the residential areas of the slave. The plantation itself took the cell form of a modern ghetto. Slaves lived in a row of shanties a few hundred yards away from "the big house" of their white masters. Separate living was automatic and organic. In a curious kind of way we could continue this parallel into our own time. We could refer to the Harlems of America as the twentieth-century slave quarters and today's "big house" would be the great, clear, free, democratic areas in each city where the white folks have their homes.

What happened in Germany from 1932 through World War II is comparable to what happened in the United States from 1620 through 1861. It may be easier to grasp understanding of the origin of segregated housing and caste feeling by looking at Germany rather than by plowing so many acres of our history. The process, within each nation, has been about the same. Hitler came in with *decrees,* with *laws,* which most of us can remember. We can recall the edicts that expropriated certain classes. The effect of this over a period of a few years was to create in the German mind the attitude that certain national, class, and religious groups had no rights which the "master race" was bound to respect. By the time the war broke out Germany had created wide national attitudes of "racial" superiority, which even now may not be eradicated, and it had established slave classes. All that is within the memory of most of us. It was done by law and force and violence and it was achieved in the economic interest of one national group over the interests of all other world nationals.

The same principle and the same approach developed in America. It arose more slowly and its pattern was more uneven, but our country worked at it for centuries rather than decades. When colonial United States evolved separatism there was no conflict with economic interests in the New World or abroad to prevent us from creating it. There was little white resistance, no labor movement, and not enough anti-slavery sentiment to prevent the rise of slavery and the establishment of caste.

The first whites and Negroes to arrive here early in the seventeenth century had had no previous contact. They may have been alien to one another and curious about each other, but they had no prejudice as we now know it. Negroes couldn't speak English, and the colonials couldn't speak African dialects, and there were other cultural differences, but caste status was unknown and mutual fear on grounds of color was non-existent. Caste had to be built, and it took laws, laws which were enforced to do it. The colonial legislatures, seeking ways of ensuring cheap labor, wrote these statutes into law, pressed their meaning into the environment.

That period saw the use of many devices for the securing of cheap labor. There were indentured white servants, for example, who, in return for their passage being paid to America, served employers for a term of years before they became free agents to sell their labor for wages. Most of us at all conversant with colonial history know that convict labor was used here too, that criminal elements exchanged jail terms abroad for the freedom to labor here, also on an indentured basis. For perhaps a few years, from 1620 through 1650, it may be that the status of Negroes varied between indentured service, slavery, and wage-labor for a few ex-indentured Negroes. But the planters, desirous of a major source for the accumulation of capital so that they might exploit the natural riches of the New World, swiftly settled upon the Negro as the most accessible and helpless source. After his seizure in violence in the slave trade, it was only a repetitive act to maintain him in the violent act of slavery. They decided that the primary available capital source was in the black 'man's labor time, which must be *completely utilized*. The other principal source for the accumulation of capital was the Indian population. Indian properties like Manhattan, "purchased" for twenty-four dollars, cornfields and other agrarian cultivations were seized and adapted to colonial needs and the Indians themselves were forced westward. The combination of whatever could be stolen from the Indians, the full labor time of the Negro (slavery), and natural resources gave the planters that start which culminated in the slave power at the height of its strength in 1861.

It was in the nature of laws that imprisoned people as slaves, that all kinds of secondary controls had to be established, laws that would prevent free movement, the formation of organizations, the holding of public meetings; and swiftly, as one of the surest means of creating a mythology, there must be laws preventing the mingling of Negro and white. All such restrictive legislation led to the segregation ordinances and landlords' agreements of our time.

Back in the days of chattel slavery it wasn't necessary to have laws on the books calling for segregation districts. The condition of the slaves in their shacks on the plantation was organic segregation. It was after the Reconstruction period that the situation began to change.

As we approached the twentieth century, Negroes began to buy property and there developed numerous places where residential lines began to crisscross, become unclear. Poor-white neighborhoods often merged with colored neighborhoods. Negroes able to buy property bought into the better home areas. Around 1900 this condition became quite widespread.

Maryland and Virginia cities established segregation ordinances around 1910 and 1912. The Virginia State Legislature passed a law in 1912 that read:

"WHEREAS the preservation of the public morals, public health, and public order in the cities and towns of this Commonwealth is endangered by the residence of white and colored peoples in close proximity to one another it is enacted that in cities and towns where this act is adopted, the entire area within the corporate limits shall be divided into 'segregation districts.' It shall be unlawful for any colored person to move into a white district, or a white person to move into a colored district. This act does not preclude persons of either race employed as servants by persons of the other race from residing on the premises of the employer."

But such enactments written into local and state law have not passed easily by the Supreme Court. The Supreme Court has ruled against such legislation. This has only driven dominant property interests to flaunt the Constitution in a different way: landowners have made deals with each other to prohibit ownership and occupancy by those rated as unacceptable. Such restrictions, specifically mentioning Negroes and Mongolians, have been written into real property deeds all over the nation. The position of the Supreme Court has been that this has been a matter of real property law rather than a constitutional matter, and therefore does not fall under the Fourteenth Amendment. The courts have decided that a deed between landowners is the action of an individual and not of a state. This decision has been given repeatedly in such cases.

We evolved a federal constitution weak enough so that in the 1850's Chief Justice Roger Taney could interpret it to mean that "a Negro has no rights which a white man is bound to respect." Then when we had a war, in good measure over this issue, we put a Fourteenth Amendment into the Constitution ostensibly taking care of human rights. State and local ordinances proceeded to batter that down. Corporations took over this amendment to protect property rights. Realty interests twisted its meaning so that they could get one Supreme Court decision after another protecting their right to draw up real property deeds with provisions excluding Negroes and other minorities from residential areas. Thus the United States Supreme Court is as guilty of misinterpretation of the Constitution today as Taney was guilty in 1857. The Supreme Court, in effect, upholds a realtor's right to discriminate.

Whatever the Fourteenth Amendment intended, with its clause that no state shall abridge the privileges or immunities of citizens, the people of color have benefited neither from its meaning nor its practice. Big realtors still see in restricting the Negro a special source for making money, as the planters saw it only a little more brutally in the early colonial period.

The increased revenue to landlords by virtue of segregated housing, which is probably the major restrictive evil, results in income over and above the rentals which would be obtainable "normally" from America if rent costs and tenancy privilege were the same for white and Negro. This extra income nationally and annually is such a large margin as to represent the profit on which much, perhaps even most, of the housing expansion in the nation is able to base itself. The Negro American, in a great measure, one that I am unable to compute accurately and swiftly, but which some economist ought to undertake to estimate, is a reservoir of capital accumulation. How so?

Restrictive housing permits realtors to charge whites for the "privilege" of living separately. *White America would do well to take note of this. It must pay heavily everywhere for the dubious exercise of exclusiveness and "supremacy."* Also, as ghettos fill up, and the demand for rooms, apartments, and houses increases, rents of the Negro people rise correspondingly and the landlord secures rentals that are much higher than would result from white occupation of the same buildings. In addition, when Negroes begin tenancy in buildings formerly white-occupied, the landlord usually abandons maintenance costs or reduces them to a minimum, and this provides another source of income.

At this point the federal courts protect realtors' private agreements to keep Negroes out of specific neighborhoods. If the courts ruled against these racial covenants such decisions might well cut deeply into the strength of, or even bankrupt, major realtors. The courts, therefore, from economic motivation and loyalty to property above all else, and from absolute need to maintain the present structure of property values, stand by the landlords.

With the person of color seized upon so brutally as a special source of income and as a check with which to balance off and maintain high rentals from white society, what is this then for the Negro but an extension of the property status which he occupied a hundred years ago, altered only in degree and form so as to fit contemporary conditions?

In the period of slavery the status of the Negro was very clear. He was a slave, or a free Negro who received very small wages

[100

for his work. No longer a chattel slave, but, in the modern conditions of Jim Crow, victimized largely by the nation's realtors, the Negro occupies a kind of mass *rent slavery* status. I am not saying this pictures his entire economic condition. I say only that this is a significant portion of his economic mis-experience, and I use the term "rent slavery" derivatively from the fundamental relationship of segregated living districts to the property owners maintaining this segregation. The term rent slavery is used in the sense that most Negroes, North and South, have this ghetto form of exploitation in common, no matter what their economic status may be and no matter how they may derive their livelihood. The Negro carries the heavy burden of segregated living on top of his other economic relationships to the nation such as wage-earner, unemployed, sharecropper, peon, professional or domestic worker, and businessman.

Until recently the Negro was engaged almost alone in an independent struggle against this phase of economic abridgement. Lately labor and interracial organizations have entered into or intensified the fight against restrictive covenants.

"JIM CROWDED" is the significant title of a circular sent to me recently by the commission on law and social action of the American Jewish Congress, which has urged support of a law prohibiting court enforcement of restrictive covenants. I believe, however, that the main message in this issue is directed at white labor, which cannot have the Negro worker as a complete wage-earning ally unless it assists unstintingly in the deliverance of the Negro from his special status as a rent slave.

CHAPTER NINE

THE EDUCATION OF WHOM?

> *"During the carpetbag regime, foisted upon the South by the radicals in Congress, millions of dollars were wasted in extravagances—like perfume and whiskey and gold-plated cuspidors for legislators. . . ."*
>
> —DR. ALLAN NEVINS and HENRY STEELE COMMAGER in *The Pocket History of the United States.*

A YOUTHFUL historian named Samuel, who considered himself a liberal, paced about in his study in a small New England town, and mused on the complexities of scholarship, historiography, and the needs of the people. He had just completed an interpretation of the course of the American nation in the period of the Civil War, and he was now confronted with a great and unanswered question.

He was confused by his discovery that the Rosetta Stone of our national history, a certain Golden Cuspidor, famous in legend was unknown in fact. All that he had studied and written was as nothing if the story of the Golden Cuspidor were to remain unverified and unconfirmed. On him, he decided, devolved the task of proving or disproving the truth or falsity of the legend, the existence or non-existence of the Golden Cuspidor. He himself was neutral and had no opinion. The Southern historians said that the Golden Cuspidor was the great fact of Reconstruction. Negro historians almost alone contended that the great fact of Negro Reconstruction was Progress and Reform. Northern historians, conservative and liberal alike, usually yawned over this phase of history, and took the word of the Confederate historians that profligacy and corruption marked the Reconstruction era as symbolized by the Golden Cuspidor. They denied or ignored that the Reconstruction was a liberation period and a time of advance in suffrage, education, economic and cultural life, as contended by the Negro historians and a handful of white allies.

Samuel, as a neutral, must go forth and find this key, this clue to what might be the coming century of understanding in the United States. He must hold in his hand the Golden Cuspidor!

Young Samuel, with the bewhiskered chin, the high hat with a band of stars around it, the blue swallow-tailed coat, and the red-and-white striped trousers that descended gracefully from his waist, paced his library with increasing ardor. Now, thought he, was the time to leave the book and the study: for him the high road and the quest for the Golden Cuspidor. If it was true, as they all declared, that the Negro legislators entered the lawmaking chambers in a spirit of luxury and profligacy, if they dressed like courtiers or sought so to dress, if, indeed, they spat into cuspidors of solid gold as one Confederate writer after another averred, then surely such durable objects must still be in existence! They might still be found in the capitols, or the museums, or in the homes of collectors, or in art galleries.

"Gold does not easily vanish," reasoned our youthful historiographer, with great common sense. "Claude Bowers," he meditated, "speaks of two hundred cuspidors for one hundred and twenty-five men. The *Documentary History of Reconstruction* attests to 'ornamental cuspidors' and 'decorated spittoons' for the legislators of South Carolina. Nordhoff avers it; Pike declares it; Ella Lonn swears it; Robert Somers tells it. Each quotes the other and swears by the other. Even Commager and Nevins, the Northern historians, repeat it."

"Find the Golden Cuspidor," said the historian to himself, and, borrowing funds from the proper foundation, he wrapped a blue cape around his shoulders, bade farewell to his wife and his forty-eight children, dashed out into the open yard into a blinding hailstorm, and strode down through his village street bound for the South on his quest for the American grail: Ye Solid Golden Cuspidor.

Thirty-five years passed, and Samuel, having wandered through every hamlet and house of the South, was in despair, for he had found no Golden Cuspidor. Nothing but brass. He was an aged man now whose hair streamed white in long tresses down about his shoulders and in whose blue eyes a weary look had settled.

Yet one day as he moved slowly into the main street of a village in the Southern state of Claghorn, and as he stopped one citizen after another to ask if he possessed the Golden Cuspidor, one townsman suddenly cried, "Thou art the man?"

"Yea, I am the man, for God's sake, tell me where it is!"

"Thou must go to the Governor of the State of Claghorn," said the citizen, with a wise twinkle in his liberal Southern eye. "It is in his possession. He shall free thee."

The doddering Samuel, faithful to his lifelong quest, reached the capitol building of Claghorn. He noticed the splendor of the stone building which housed the governor. Two gentlemen of color, stationed at the entrance, graciously took the aged scholar and seeker within. Samuel, who was barefoot and sore, sank his feet into the soft carpet that led down a long corridor to the governor's office. The old man now entered the luxurious, air-cooled room in which the great governor sat before his desk.

And the eyes of the venerable scholar were riveted upon what he saw there; for he gazed at a governor on whose head was a crown of gold. It was a great golden crown, shaped like a cuspidor, an ancient cuspidor of the Reconstruction period, the very cuspidor into which the Negro legislators were said to have spat, and there it rested easily on the head of the Claghorn governor and the governor smiled and the gold glittered, and suddenly old Samuel perceived the truth. . . .

The golden crown started to melt before his eyes. It melted in streams of warm gold that poured down the face and shoulders of the governor who sat immutable, as if unaware what was happening. Samuel saw then the Golden Cuspidor was but the ascent to power of the class represented by the governor, and this class and this governor were bathing in this very gold, transmuted, like alchemy, from the crushing of the Negro legislators and people, into this handsome building, this handsome governor, and this handsome crown.

The gold now melted entirely over the governor, covering his outer garments and penetrating within, too, so that, in the eyes of Samuel, the Golden Cuspidor was nothing less than the heart and soul and body of the governor himself. All was bathed in the gold of power, and now Samuel turned away, and moved out of the capitol knowing that he had found what he had sought.

The foregoing allegory is not far-fetched as a description of the way in which Northern historians have accepted and reflected the compromise which the Republican Party worked out in 1876 with the Democrats. From the time when it became correct and fashionable to "heal the wounds" between the white North and the white South, most Northern historians have decided to accept the Southern view that the Negro and carpetbag legislatures were "corrupt." This was preferable to showing the progressive reforms in land redistribution, the introduction of wage labor in place of slave labor, the opening of public schools and extension of education to all, and other reforms sought by the Reconstruction legislature. Northern historians, living and dead, including practically all of the liberals such as Charles A. Beard, David S. Muzzey, Alvin

Harlow, James F. Rhodes, William A. Dunning, Allan Nevins, and H. S. Commager have reflected the Southern viewpoint of the Reconstruction. The method has been either to accept fully the Reconstruction as a "corrupt" period or to try to appear neutral by saying that national interest was re-harmonized and everything that occurred (re-suppression of the Negro) happened for the best.

When Mrs. Eleanor Roosevelt was briefing British war brides in London as they embarked for America, she warned them that "In certain parts of the United States, unreasoning prejudices exist, dating from certain history books that have never been changed." She meant Southern history books, but unhappily her statement is just as true for most history books used in such a great metropolitan center as New York City. Furthermore, the prejudices stem from far more deep-seated institutions than books. The books reflect primarily the institution of political compromise.

I have preferred to tell the story of distortion in textbooks used throughout the nation in the form of an allegory rather than to attempt any detailed examination of what is wrong with them. It happens that I did conduct such a survey for a period of about three months in the columns of the *Defender,* mentioning the vagaries of a number of typical books. Actually the job of reviewing all the textbooks in use nationally and pointing out their shortcomings is on the monumental side; it is its own book; the most that I can do here is to suggest the main outlines of their fallacies.

In general, the books in use throughout the North and South, in grade schools, high schools, and colleges, err in the same way. They omit the Negro's enormous economic contribution in the colonial life of the nation; they distort and misinterpret the role of the Negro in the Civil War; and they deliberately take a Confederate position of attacking the Negro-Republican Reconstruction regime when democracy was more of a reality in the nation than it is today. Take just one typical book that has been widely

[106

used in the nation's schools in recent years, David Saville Muzzey's *History of the American People*. Muzzey does not even accord the Negro people the courtesy of spelling Negro with a capital *N*. Throughout the word is used with a small *n* and the Negro is not even listed in the index. Muzzey, like most of today's white historians of Reconstruction, follows trustingly the Confederate historical approach evolved in the 1890's and at the turn of the century.

One way that the Confederates attacked the Reconstruction legislatures and made their attack sound credible was to list the furnishings of the various state capitols used by the Negro and Republican legislators, and charge these legitimate expenditures to waste and extravagance. None of the Confederate historians or their Northern followers of today, who are quick to list the lounges, armchairs, desks, mirrors, tables, and cuspidors used in the capitols (most of which were necessities), ever mention the waste, extravagance, decadence, and unnecessary luxury of the plantation homes, or the profligacy of the entire system of slavery, or the violence and corrupt betrayal of the Reconstruction. Muzzey, like the others, becomes enthusiastic in the listing of the objects purchased to equip the capitols, but is calm when he discusses the slave trade.

This type of historiography is as unfair as it would be to criticize President Truman's administration because the White House underwent expensive repairs in 1946, which is a fact. I daresay that if some enemy of President Truman were to get a look at the bills listing the items purchased for the White House in 1946 the Truman administration could be made to seem corrupt, wasteful, and extravagant *on that account*. I know, as a newspaperman, that such a technique is a frequent resort when it is necessary, on any grounds, to score off one's opponent. If this tactic could be forgiven the Confederates, on the grounds that they had an organic bias to defend, it can only mean that many of today's best-known historians have forfeited their right to a liberal rating in their

107]

approach to the Negro and to Reconstruction, the *essential struggle* of recent American history.

I had some words with historian Allan Nevins about this. He said that he thought current histories could make some "slight revisions" in handling the Reconstruction. He wasn't ready to go as far as Howard Fast, however. It happens that Fast was the first historian of the present century to bring to a wide, general public the true story of the Reconstruction (in his *Freedom Road*). But as late as 1943, Nevins' and Commager's *Pocket History of the United States,* quoted at the outset of this chapter, read no differently in interpretation of the Reconstruction than the Confederate histories from which it derived its viewpoint.

If I seem to have singled out the Nevins-Commager tract for special attention, then so be it, for these are the younger historians, the carriers-on of "liberalism" in historiography, and the obligation to face the facts and cease pursuing the unholy grail of the Golden Cuspidor falls upon them.

The misinformation in textbooks goes out to both white and Negro students nationally. Yet this is only one facet in the chain reaction of misunderstanding affecting the educational structures of the land as a result of Jim Crow. Basic to the attitudes of difference between Negro and white is the arrangement of separate schools in the South and in some places in the North.

How this contradiction works out so as to retard the South— and the entire nation—is best understood in the story of the acrobat who could twist his right leg around his neck while keeping his left leg around the leg of a chair. The acrobat decided that if he could just manage to twist his left leg around his neck as well, in addition to circling the chair with it, then he'd really be performing some trick. He did it too, but his strained muscular system froze up and he remains in that position to this day.

Such is the condition of the South with its acrobatic attempt to maintain two school systems, one for white and one for colored.

[108

THE EDUCATION OF WHOM?

The South, to begin with, is a poverty-stricken area of the nation. On top of this it has sought to pay for two school systems. To complicate that matter the law states that the separate accommodations for the Negro shall be of the same or equal facilities as those granted to the white. The poverty of state and local educational budgets makes that impossible to attain. What happens is that the Negro schools are as dumpy-looking as many of the shacks the Negroes live in. Then, as a sequel, the white schools are impoverished from a lack of books, teachers, furnishings, and morale. But the caste system is maintained. It stays frozen, like the acrobat.

The South is in the position of that gargoyle acrobat who, with his head striking out oddly from its tangle of chairs, legs, and neck, eyes popping, looks at the world unable to talk but trying to say, "See, I did it!"

Segregated schools are no recent development. Like almost everything else in the contemporary Jim Crow framework, the origins of the system date back to the colonial slave period. Negroes were securing separate instruction in reading and writing in Charleston, South Carolina, as early as 1695, and a full-fledged school for Negroes was established in the Carolinas in 1744. Some slaveholders believed in granting limited education to certain slaves in order that these slaves, in turn, might teach reading and writing to the masters' children. But, largely, the object of slavery was to prevent Negroes from securing education, just as it is a major object of national policy, often bluntly stated, to this day. Describing the status of the Negro in relation to education under slavery, Frederick Douglass remarked: "Whatever of comfort is necessary for him for his body or soul that is inconsistent with his being property is carefully wrested from him, not only by public opinion but by the laws of the country. . . . He is deprived of education. God gave him an intellect; the slaveholder declares it shall not be cultivated." That was the slaveholders' policy and it was the forerunner of segregated education today. Says the Southern senator, "If we can't keep learnin' from him altogether, we'll make it as bad for him as we can." When Columbia University keeps a rigid admission quota for Negroes and other minorities, it flirts with the educational policy of the early American slave mart. When noted liberals place so much emphasis on vocational and farm training for Negroes, they express, not their good will, but their desire to retain the Negro as the source of commodity production that he has always been. Actually vocational and industrial training for the Negro in the past and today may be his greatest asset, for it has enabled him to make ever closer alliance with his principal political assistant, the white worker, but it is interesting to observe that motivations for urging industrial training on Negroes have depended upon the class interests of those urging it. Frederick Douglass spoke out as early as 1853 in favor of an Industrial College for Negroes because he saw political possibilities and economic certainties in a mechanically skilled Negro laboring class, but in the case of Hans Kaltenborn, an example in our own day, who also urges that kind of training for Negroes, it is because he fears the political advance of the Negro that might result from liberal arts, legal, or scientific education. "I believe so much in teaching trades and vocations," he told me, "and not assuming that a higher education is beneficial, because unless we have opportunities, it creates discontent. If I were trying to advise Negroes to be of constructive use I'd say to train to be scientific farmers, skilled artisans, teachers. There are enough Negro politicians, orators, lawyers."

The exclusion of Negroes in the slave period had been so total that in the transition to Reconstruction the progressive forces apparently did not have the strength to immediately effect integrated schooling. The abolitionists and anti-slavers who entered Reconstruction work as soon as they could labored under great handicaps, handicaps imposed by the vacillation of the federal government, Confederate opposition, and Uncle Tom elements among Negroes themselves. The freedmen, hitherto entirely denied elementary education, had to take advantage of new-won

[110

gains as swiftly as possible. They were grouped together in make-shift schools and started on their way. There was no fertile situation at the outset in which their learning could be linked with concurrent teaching of whites. Meantime the Southern forces were already regirding to maintain traditional separatism, and in this they had the assistance of suppliant Negro preachers. The effects were felt in the extension of the public-school system that evolved in the post-Civil War period in the South. In Virginia, for example, in 1869, when the first system of schools free to all was opened, it was on a basis of separate schools for Negro and white. The same process more or less repeated itself in the other Southern states.

Consider Alabama, where clay and caste abound in equal quantities. In 1832 it was a crime punishable by a $250 to $500 fine to instruct a Negro in reading or writing. Today official Alabama does whatever damage it can by arranging that the Negro schools secure as little money as possible and by rushing the Negro child from the school into the field or factory as soon as possible. If, through a complex of political and economic pressures, this object fails, and the Negro does get through grade and high schools anyway, then he has to get his higher education in a segregated Negro college, preferably one run by a Negro minister. In fact, it was pointed out to me recently that at one time practically every Negro college was headed by a Negro preacher and that a number of the leading Negro colleges right now are headed by ex-preachers. Here the theory is that a religionist, being a peaceloving man, will keep his students pacified.

I said earlier that restricted housing may be the fundamental evil of Jim Crow, that from separate living districts there arise the diverse genii of misunderstanding. If I wanted to split hairs over the main sources of our unique system of "Two Worlds," I might also say that the processes of separate education are as fundamental to the production of misunderstanding as separate living districts. Leon Ransome, chairman of the Committee for Racial

Democracy in Washington, at an "I Am An American Day" rally, made the statement that discrimination has its genesis in the public schools, as a result of which "we can't grow up to know each other and to discover that we are all Americans." There should be no argument about which is worse, segregated housing or segregated schools. Syphilis should not be preferable to leprosy, or leprosy to syphilis.

In the face of this overall evil of separate schools, any examination of the Negro school or college itself is but to touch the sorest spot of all. I have neither taught nor been taught in one of these "institutions" and therefore cannot give a personal documentation of the situation. Anyone interested in the unhappy details can get them from Dr. Horace Mann Bond's *Negro Education in Alabama*. They can also get a hint of what, and what alone, can change the system in the last paragraph of Dr. Bond's book, where he says: "To essay a prophecy of major changes in the immediate future is to anticipate a change in the social and economic order as revolutionary as that catastrophe which, from 1861–1865, destroyed the institution of chattel slavery, and led to the wholly revolutionary acceptance of the principle that Negro children should be educated at public expense." Throughout the writings of the most advanced Negro Americans I always find a yearning for a New Reconstruction period, and I am with them in this aspiration.

But neither the misinformation in history textbooks nor separate schooling *per se* touches the basic issue of American education and the Negro. It is one thing, and a correct thing, to expose and oppose distortion in textbooks used by white and Negro; and it is right and inevitable that separate schooling must everywhere be subjected to the ridicule which it deserves, but while these processes go on, they must be understood as secondary phenomena. That great host of liberals who feel they contribute to dissolving Jim Crow in America by benevolently urging more funds for Negro education are backing a horse that comes in fifth. It is fine to bet on the horse, for at least it is in the race, but where the fault lies and where the main force must be directed is best illustrated in a story told by Alfred E. Smith, a raconteur for the *Defender* who describes the meeting of two Negro citizens on a Birmingham street:

The first citizen asks, "Well, how'er your white folks coming along?"

And the second answers, "Oh, we're educatin' them and they're comin' along slowly, but they've got a long ways to go."

That is the nub and the truth of the situation. That illustrates what is wrong with the educational system and who needs to be educated. It is not the Negro American who suffers from the malady of white supremacy and needs to be cured of it. The delusion of essential superiority is the exclusive possession of large sections of the white-skinned populace, and the main drives in educational, economic, and political change must be directed at uprooting this network of fetishism in the white American outlook and practice. This is now a widely acknowledged fact. Like a cloudburst the whole system of white supremacy has come down from the period of slavery, leaving in its wake a flood of segregated institutions. There must be and there is an all-front fight against each of these areas of discrimination. But the answer to Jim Crow cannot be found within the educational structures of society alone. Neither correct textbooks by themselves, nor an increase in nonsectarian schools carry more than a partial answer. Struggle for correction in these arenas America must, but only as an aspect of the overall attack on the cancerous Jim Crow economy. Reading and writing in the larger sense must still be taught to white America, for, as the Negro experience proves, the ABC's of human understanding are not written into our institutions. We must clearly realize that if not one Negro in the land could spell his name it would still be the vast millions of white Americans who remained the untaught.

CHAPTER TEN

THE FALLACY OF "RACE"

"RACE" thinking permeates America everywhere. It is like a contagion. A German-Jewish refugee woman, my neighbor, driven out of Germany because of her "race," complains to me that she doesn't want to go to a certain swimming pool because "there are too many colored there." She has been here three years and has discovered America.

I walk along 125th Street in Harlem and I hear one Negro greet another. Instead of saying, "Shake hands," he smiles and utters, "Give me some skin, brother."

I have a talk with Sono Osato, a dancer in Broadway shows. Her grandfather, named Fitzpatrick, settled in and helped build Canada. She has Irish, French, and everything else of Europe in her veins. Her father was a Japanese-American. She looks Japanese herself with her yellowish complexion, large black eyes, and long black hair. She was Nebraska-born. Now tell me what is the American type?

I go into the home of a Negro family. It is a large family. The father is white-colored and blond-haired, and the mother is black. Both would be "Negroes" to the average American. They have eight children. Each one has a different shade. They range all the way from jet-black to high blond. Each resembles one parent or the other in facial features. Tell me what is white and what is black?

THE FALLACY OF "RACE"

I read that a man named Wendell Willkie made a trip around the world, came back, and wrote a book called *One World*. Then I go to my office and I spend a day dealing with my particular brand of facts and come away at night saying to myself, "One World, Two Colors."

I meet up with Fredi Washington, a columnist for the *People's Voice*. She once played Peola in *Imitation of Life,* the story of the plight of a mulatto girl supposedly belonging neither to one color group nor to the other. She looks white and Irish to me. I come away confused after a talk with her. She reasons out of the interest of the Negro group, lives with Negroes, and is a "Negro" by all American standards. I ask her questions about "passing" in the white world, which she can do. "I don't wear a sign saying I'm Negro," she explains. I keep thinking about it and finally reach the conclusion that her viewpoint cannot be understood in terms of color, but only in terms of historical institutions of segregation.

A Negro goes to Congress from Harlem and his name is Powell. He is lighter than a senator who attacks him for his color! A Negro who is a blond is the head of the National Association for the Advancement of Colored People. In addition to the fact that he is a Negro who looks white he represents blacks and his name is White. Take it from there and tell me about "race."

In the small town of Upright, Virginia, three white families totaling about fifty people belong neither to the white nor black communities. Late in the last century the rumor got around that there was "Negro blood" in this blond, Anglo-descended group. They were ostracised. Today eighteen white children denied entrance to the white school and not wanting to go to the Negro school are growing up illiterate in a new "Tobacco Road." The situation has been in the Virginia courts for decades. Color, thy contradictions are legion!

I go to a meeting of the Haitian Patriotic Union where I am scheduled to speak in celebration of the ousting of dictator Lescot of Haiti. Half the speeches are in French, for most of the audience is made up of French-speaking Haitians. But some of the "Negroes" look like white Frenchmen. One of the speakers greets the French-speaking Haitians in the name of the Spanish-speaking West Indians. He is introduced by an English-speaking Jamaican, and all are referring to themselves variously as Africans, Negroes, West Indians, Americans, and French-, English-, and Spanish-speaking citizens of color. Occasionally the word "race" pokes its nose in. I see every shade of color, hear every European tongue, listen to music of all the national groups in the West Indies, and the meeting winds up with Roger Baldwin's telling the wildly applauding assemblage that some day "The colored people will put the white man in his place."

When I see such contradictions as these I get the feeling the country is literally sick, possibly mad, and that it may need a medical diagnosis. I have often thought of Jim Crow as a kind of national illness, as an infection, and I have wondered whether it could be understood and opposed in medical terms. (Any terms to reach ever wider groups is my policy.) So I buttonhole my old friend, Albert Deutsch, psychiatrist and sociologist, and I say: "Albert, I think I've isolated a new germ, the *blanc supremacoccus* bacillus. What can we do about it?"

He gets it immediately and, like a Doctor of Human Understanding, he analyzes the nation this way: "The fundamental national contradiction—that is, the contradition between our doctrine of equal rights and our practice of unequal treatment—has been rapidly coming toward a showdown. It is making millions of whites very uncomfortable. That is the greatest of the many contradictions in American attitudes toward 'race,' which has tended to create a schizoid or split-personality culture. The schizoid personality is a bundle of inner conflicts and contradictions." Then he tells me what these are, which is what I myself have been discussing heretofore, and he concludes: "I am not saying that the answer to racial friction and discrimination lies in psychiatric treatment for the whole population. The causes of racial prejudices and discrimination are deeply rooted in our economic system and in the insecurities that bedevil great numbers of people. These insecurities create fears and hates that cloud the mind and get people with fundamentally common interests to hate and fight one another. The fundamental solution for the so-called 'race problem' lies in economic and social reforms that can be built upon a secure and healthy citizenry, but the path toward this goal can be cleared toward speedy action if whites would come to grips with their own consciences and ruthlessly check up each belief with the objective facts."

I liked that. What are the "objective facts"? I think they are to be found where Deutsch suggested they were: "deeply rooted in our economic system."

Gunnar Myrdal, in his *An American Dilemma,* states that the Negro problem is not an easy one to solve. "It is a tremendous task for theoretical research to find out why the Negro's status is what it is," he says, acknowledging that he does not know. Then he proceeds to point out that it is a moral, a mental matter. "We started," he says, "by stating the hypothesis that the Negro problem has its existence in the American's mind. There the decisive struggle goes on. It is there the changes occur."

He is, of course, off the track. Myrdal fails to point out that the wrong may be attributable to the historic development of our economic and political institutions, because this would mean we might need some economic and political changes. Therefore, his huge two-volume work is almost devoid of historical examination. He deals, in the main, with contemporary white and Negro attitudes, and winds up saying it is a matter of conscience, a matter of practicing what we have preached. He omits a three-hundred-year history of major-party political compromise, with the Negro as the goat. He fails to explain the evolution of the "race" concept as a purely American production *in order to control and subjugate the Negro.* It is that evolutionary process I wish to indicate. . . .

When the country was first colonized the main need of the Dutch and English shipping companies was for an agrarian laboring class to cultivate the soil, cut down the trees, and build settlements. John Rolfe, historian of the first Virginia settlement, complained of the difficulty of establishing a working class out of the white colonists. "They would all be Keisers, none inferior to the other," he wrote, suggesting that what was needed was a class of "inferiors," that is, workers, servants, slaves. The problem arose: Where to get them?

According to John Rolfe, when the settlers and the Indians clashed in 1622, the colonists were urged to war on the natives without mercy, with the single exception that they should preserve younger Indians "whose bodies may by labor and service become profitable." Here was expressed again the main need for a profit-creating class. Here was no moral, social, anthropological, or other concern for the Indian as a "race" or "color," but solely, and crudely, as the age-old potential workhand.

For a generation after 1619 the English colonists used two sources of cheap labor. One was the vagrant, often criminal or otherwise arrestable, class of London that could be put into indentured-servant status, and the other was the African who could be captured or bought at a minimum cost. By 1650 or 1660 the African began to be preferred by the shippers, planters, and slave traders because he represented practically total profit. When the Company of Royal Adventurers was formed in London in 1622, sponsored by the Queen Dowager and the Duke of York, the royalty wasn't interested a whit in the ethnology of the African, but was concerned with him solely as an agricultural worker. The war in Africa was to capture slaves and fieldhands; neither the thinking nor acting was in the terms of "race" in the sense that employers of today, on job application forms, ask an applicant's race. Profits alone determined the capture of Africans, and questions of anthropology, sociology, and morality entered later *as a means of control of the slave labor supply*.

An important step in the involvement of the entire colonial public in the development of slavery, with a consequent "racial" attitude being created occurred in 1698. That year the slave trade was opened to the public, and anyone with a ship and sufficient money to get to Africa and enough men and gunpowder or trinkets for exchange with which to secure a hundred or so slaves, could participate in the traffic. Compare that with the means practiced by large corporations in our own day when they allow the middle and working classes to buy stocks and bonds. In the same way that the general public is led to believe that it has a stake in corporate wealth and the economic structure of which corporations are a part—only to be cleaned out during periods of stockmarket crashes—so the colonial public, allowed to take part in the slave trade, found itself afterward saddled with a system of slavery. This early permeation of the public mind with the slave institution forms the ancestral base, in the main, for our current institutions of Jim Crow.

It was at about the same time that the British Crown stepped into the picture by collecting taxes on newly imported slaves. With this government "take" there came legal and official sanction for slavery on a high level. In such a process we see the direct source of current state control of the Negro in the South today, and of Congressional indifference to such legislation as the Fair Employment Practices measures. The point is that the profit motive, beginning with shippers, planters, slave traders, and the colonial assemblies, spread to the stage of Crown taxation itself, thus laying the basis in deeds for a later need to rationalize, justify, and defend slavery. The more such processes developed the more there spread the myth of the Negro's "racial inferiority" as the justification for such processes, and the clearer became the concept of "race."

Throughout the era when the economic base was established for rearing theories of "race," secondary phenomena appeared to give social sanction to the institution. The clergy sustained this orgy of profit-taking by contending that slavery made "Christians of infidels, and useful servants of savages." Slave captains could get up in church and thank God that an omnipresent Providence was "pleased to bring to this land of freedom another cargo of benighted heathen to enjoy the blessings of gospel dispensation." In such a thanksgiving as that, uttered three hundred years ago, one can see the root form of the great contradiction in the land today: that freedom and slavery may exist side by side. That is why one can hear a Baptist or Methodist preacher in a smart Fifth Avenue church today talking about the "race" occupying Baptist and Methodist churches on the back streets of Harlem.

Throughout the South one encounters the pious declaration that the Negro is entitled to "separate but equal accommodations." The separate accommodations of the Negro are usually filthy, whether in trains, schools, lavatories, or residential areas. What is the origin of this "racial" separation? Descriptions of the holds of slave ships that sailed the seas in the colonial period provide the answers. While white crews walked freely on deck, "the holds were partitioned off into racks, about two feet by six, and fitted with leg irons and bars." That was economy construction, like the Negro schoolhouse of today.

The pattern of contemporary Jim Crow comes down from slavery almost like a blueprint. For example, when slaves first arrived in Virginia they were subjected to a period of instruction so as to learn subservience to white authority. Specially trained Negroes called "bellwethers" put the new slave arrivals through these paces. They also taught the slaves "black English," which was elementary conversation that could make them understood to overseers and make the latter understood to them. There was the historic origin of the modern "Uncle Tom" or quisling Negro who is at the service of white masters in holding down and betraying his kinsmen of color. There also is the origin of those minor differences of pronunciation and accent which characterize the speech of Negroes in some parts of the South to this day.

The lynch *motif* of the South stems from the earliest times. In

1627 some West Indian captives rebelled from slave labor with settlers, and ran to the interior, hiding with Indians. The colonial leaders ruled that these runaways were so great a danger that they should be taken and hanged. But the runaways were not dangerous because of their color or the curl of their hair. They were dangerous because they opposed the principle of slave labor. With the passage of time and the transformation of chattel slavery into Jim Crow, a mythology of special attitudes toward and about the Negro merged with the developing pattern of socio-economic exclusion. What resulted was the evolving fetishism of "race" which now appears as a strong element in clashes and lynchings. Those who attack the Negro, whether for his "race" or for his real or alleged offenses, do not know the historic propulsions behind their deeds. Such culprits become the projected puppets of the two antithetical social classes, Negro and white, living alongside each other and contending with and against each other. Actually the real content of an attack on Negroes today, no matter what its outward "racial" form or immediate cause may seem to be, is still directed against the rebellion of the Negro from the pattern historically assigned to him as cheap labor, whether under chattel slavery at one time or Jim Crow now.

How morality crossed swords occasionally with economics and how economics won is shown in the ruling of the Virginia General Assembly in 1667 that the baptism of the Negro did not alter his status as a slave. Morality could not stand in the way of profits. Christianity must be compromised that agriculture might be cultivated.

When Gunnar Myrdal says, therefore, that "the status accorded the Negro in America represents nothing less than a century-long lag of public morals," he is ignoring the first two centuries of American history when there was no lag in the accumulation of property by the settler leaders at the expense of all morality and all concern for the Negro as a human being.

It was this failure to view the Negro as a human being, and

instead the persistent view of him as a source of profit and a "machine" for hard labor, which gave rise to the rationalization that the African was "an inferior race." The principle of special treatment for the Negro in all phases of living created another principle, that of *permeation*. With the entire social system, including even the layout of residential communities, so organized as to focus attention on the Negro as a special creature, it was inevitable that in both white and Negro consciousnesses there would develop attitudes of difference. These attitudes, turning like a wheel around all the phenomena of living, spelled out "r-a-c-e." Color, the principal possession of the Negro in the evolution of this misconception, was the ethnological peg on which the economic burden was fastened and "race" created.

In the foregoing I have suggested how only a few of these processes, typical ones, worked out. If one were to pick up Elizabeth Donnan's *Documents Illustrative of the History of the Slave Trade in America,* one would find these illustrations multiplied a hundred times. The confessions, letters, diaries, and logs of the slave traders and captains show the origin of modern "racial" attitudes in a struggle for profit. The slave trade continued year after year for two hundred years, permeating the rising nation with its implications. Colonial legislatures reaffirmed their restrictive laws for an even longer period, continuing until this day and further deepening the national pattern of "Two Worlds." White churchmen went their own way and carefully planted Negro churches in Negro neighborhoods, operating with the perfection of farmers who know the right soil for the right crop. Every compulsion in society conspired to place the African, and later the Negro American, into molds of exclusion, separation, and submergence. A way of putting it would be, "If the Negro is a race, then Americans manufactured that race."

With such an inordinate historic pressure as this operating on both Negro and white Americans perennially for more than three hundred years it would have been miraculous if a new "race" had not evolved! What we call today the colored "race" originated in a complex of what the Negro was robbed of abroad: Africa; and what he was denied here: America. Cheated of Africa and denied America, he has been so relegated from the mainstream of white national life that it has been easy, even natural, for white Americans to look at him and say, "A black race, inferior too." The Negro was placed to one side like a black crow shunned by other birds. That, in fact, is how the term Jim Crow originated, as I understand it, and that is why the term expresses the whole historical institution of the Negro's early slavery and contemporary rejection. Today we call this individual variously a Negro, a "race," a colored man, a second-class citizen, a nation, a victim of Jim Crow. In the period of slavery the slaveholders put their plantation brand on the Negro and one could *see* it. Today the Negro carries such a brand just as genuinely as he did then, only now one has to *understand* it; and it reads simply, "Race. Made in the U.S.A."

These are the historical roots of what we call today the system of Jim Crow. Such conclusions as these imply more than changing people's minds, as Mr. Myrdal suggests we undertake to do during the next two generations. Such origins of Jim Crow, showing roots deep in the desire to accumulate wealth, mean that economic and political solutions must be offered rather than "moral" changes or "educational" approaches alone.

Mr. Myrdal says that the decisive struggle takes place in people's minds. I say that it has already taken place in the streets of America. Decisive struggle over the Negro took place at Gettysburg and in hundreds of slave revolts and great migrations. It takes place at Washington and at state capitols; it occurs during political demonstrations (sometimes miscalled "riots"). It takes place in the conflict of capital and labor, and it occurs in political and legal spheres, as it is taking place right now in the major parties and in the Supreme Court, and in all basic substructures of society. It is the conflict in the social-political areas that is decisive, that changes people's minds and "nature" and "morality."

123]

Those who ask for "moral" changes want no economic changes. Those who see in "education" the total answer do not want the Negro issue to take its rightful place in politics.

An example of how the Negro lives with "race" from moment to moment was brought to me by John Robert Badger, a *Defender* columnist, who is a light-complexioned Negro, but so light and redhaired he might be taken for a brother of Sinclair Lewis. Badger, who writes out of the interest of the Negro group for a Negro newspaper, was complaining to me that Negroes didn't recognize him on sight as Negro.

We were walking along 125th Street at the time and there was no reaction from passers-by to indicate anything other than that we were both white. I remarked, "Trouble with you, Badger, you haven't got enough *melanin* in your system."

"That's it," he added, "not enough melanin." And we laughed.

Our laugh was at the mythology of "race" and "Negro." Science has long since explained that dark skin coloring is merely the presence in the system of the brown chemical substance called melanin. People who are very dark have much of it. Lighter persons have less. Blonds have very little. Albinos, who may be found among all color groups, have none. John Badger, "Negro," emerged the possessor of less melanin than I.

It would probably not be a very difficult project (nor a sensible, nor a necessary one) for scientists to isolate some extract of melanin, find means of safely applying it to white people, and inject it into any blond who wanted to get a permanent tan. One could then make Lana Turner look the same color as Lena Horne in a few weeks. My point is that a simple chemical element has been used by pressure groups throughout the Western world for centuries as a base upon which to rear a whole structure of supremacist beliefs and establish a labor reservoir.

One of the best illustrations I know of how the term "race" is being canceled out in our time is in the widespread use of the term "interracial." I have used this word throughout the book. Is this a contradiction? Of course it is, but it is one I have to deal with. Anthropologist Gene Weltfish explained it to me this way: "We have to rob the word 'race' of its meaning. Until we do so rob it, we have to go on using it." Look at the historical process:

First we create a word and an idea, "race," and exalt it to a position where it has as distinct a meaning, *in our country*, as "time" or "space." But just as time and space are artificial, man-made concepts which have acted as mechanical aids to science, and even as these concepts have been transformed in our time, so, in semantics and in life, we are busily trying to negate the dangerous factors in the term "race" by putting the nullifier "inter" before it. Here we are taking an essentially negative, harsh, rigid term, "race," and robbing it of some of its inoculated reality. It is quite a somersault, yet it is being performed daily throughout the nation in thousands of actions. I have performed that social-semantic somersault throughout this book. Such processes are eroding the system of Jim Crow—but so slowly!

I have neither studied nor extensively read in the sphere of anthropology. Nor do I consider myself an ethnologist. Yet I remember that Dr. Margaret Mead, the ethnologist, told me that to be such a scientist "you have to undergo the shock of trying to take a totally different culture into your system." I suppose that something of that sort has happened to me, quite without design but in the nature of my work, and owing to my constant association with Negroes and with Harlem's communal life over a period of years. As a reporter-participant in the life and objectives of that community I have been able to measure what I have seen among Negroes against what I have heard about them all my life. This has led me to doubt and finally to repudiate practically all popular conceptions of what Negroes are and what "race" is.

Actually I have been able to learn very little about what is "Negro," "white," or "racial" by studying complexions, nose shapes, personal mannerisms, ghetto customs. In my case the "shock" is the overall fact that greets me each time I look at Harlem: that is, its inordinate socio-economic sublagation from the rest of America. That realization compelled me to seek in American history the answer to "why the Negro's status is what it is," and I believe that there I have found it. The roots of the tree of Jim Crow are to be found in the slave trade, the slave plantations, the repressive legal system of the colonial assemblies, the early struggle for restrictive legislation in marriage relations, education, and housing, and the conscious misuse of a false ethnology based on the Negro's color to create subordinate concepts of "white" and "Negro" so-called "races" within the framework of the human race. Strictly speaking, there are neither Negro nor white people except as we have reared a Frankensteinian monster in our midst and are willing to live with it.

Remembering that the substructure of modern racist ideas lies deep in the early settlers' desire to carve an empire, what is interesting and a little flabbergasting is the great superstructure of myths, mis-notions, lies, disharmonies, and clash situations which have arisen to plague us in our time. Like an exploded atom bomb, whose clouds of smoke have become something other than uranium and rise in the sky as many-natured gases, so "race" moves, cloudlike, over and through the American scene, the end-result of what the slave society bequeathed.

I have seen enthnologists and anthropologists plowing their way around Harlem, examining Negroes as if they were curios, trying to find in their faces, features, and colorings the answer to those questions, when the answer lay historically within the white man's two back pockets, in one of which he kept his revolver and in the other his purse. Professor Albert Einstein once interpreted this limited "superiority" to me: "Of course I do not believe in any superiority of the white world. The white world possesses a certain technical superiority only, and 'white supremacy' itself is only a product of this technical superiority. This does not touch on human values."

The rise and fall of ideas of "race" is itself a commentary on the vanity of the American conception of two domestic "races," the white and the black. In 1883, according to Noah Webster, ethnologists were greatly divided about the number of "races" in the world, the estimates ranging from three to eleven. Also "race" was defined at that time amorphously as "Descendant of a common ancestor, a family, tribe, people, or a nation believed or presumed to belong to the same stock; a lineage; a breed. . . ." Since then we have had two world wars, Wendell Willkie has evolved his "One World" conception, only four different blood types have been demonstrated and they may be found in each so-called "race," and there should be no doubt by now that the main fact is that there is only one "race," the human race—and that all the rest, color and curl of the hair and local customs, are minor mutations of the main fact.

Originally the letters spelling out *n-e-g-r-o* were no more than the Spanish and Portuguese for the word "black." When the Spanish and Portuguese slave traders returned to Europe with African slaves they said simply, in their own tongues, "Here are blacks." These Mediterranean derivations, in turn, traced back to the spelling *n-i-g-e-r*, which was Latin for "black." In French the word is spelled *n-o-i-r*. We took the Spanish and Portuguese word for the color black, and built a people, a "race," a system, a separate nation, and a mythology upon it. In South Africa the dark-skinned native is not called a "Negro" but a Kaffir. I mention that because I know how the American's mind works on this question. To him the "Negro" is a fixed thing. The Africans are Negro, the West Indians are Negro, the mixed Brazilians would be Negro to him, and dark-skinned Americans are Negro. He thinks the world, with its current meaning, always existed and always will. He does not know how swiftly history can sweep a tide and an idea onto the shore, and how equally swiftly another tide can sweep it away. That there is now, in America, a submerged group called the "Negro" is, however, a fact of daily living. No progress whatever can be made in behalf of either the oppressed Negro or the haunted white man by attempting to contend with the issue in terms of the false and clashing conceptuality of "race." I am inclined to agree with that astute abolitionist and orator of a century ago, Wendell Phillips, who looked upon the Negro mass in the South as a nation. Most Negroes still live in the South and still retain a social and political entity so comparable to nationhood that, as a unifying force, this may constitute the most practical political leverage they possess.

Those who have freely used the terms "race," "white," and "Negro" in attempting to describe historic relations between the Jim Crowers and the Jim Crowed might do well to realize what the so-called Negroes consider themselves.

I think that this was best expressed in an address prepared by three Negroes, L. S. Berry, William V. Turner, and R. D. Wiggins, never widely known to Americans and unhonored and unsung by historiography. They were the committee in charge of preparing an address of a Colored Convention to the people of Alabama during the Reconstruction period. Their address appeared in the *Daily State Sentinel*, published in Mobile, on May 21, 1867, when Negro freedom was at its height, hope was at its highest, and the likelihood of complete liberation was nearer for the people of color than at any time before. They put it this way, in disposing of what their status was, in disposing of "race":

". . . . All legal distinctions between the races are now abolished. The word white is stricken from our laws, and every privilege which white men were formerly permitted to enjoy, merely because they were white men, now that word is stricken out, we are entitled to on the ground that we are men. Color can no longer be pleaded for the purpose of curtailing privileges, and every public right, privilege and immunity is enjoyable by every individual member of the public. . . . The law no longer knows white nor black, but simply men, and consequently we are entitled to ride in public conveyances, hold office, sit on juries and do everything else

[128

which we have in the past been prevented from doing solely on the ground of color. . . ."

That is what the Jim Crowed want, as all would do well to note. When the law knows *but simply men* the institutions of Jim Crow will have ended, "race" will have become a myth like witch-craft, white and black will be for artists' palettes and not for ways of living, "Negro" may again become but the Spanish word for a color, and man's hatred for man on a basis of color will wither away and men to each other be *but simply men*. As in the Recon-struction period, when the foregoing was enunciated, this remains the objective of the Jim Crowed mass, and the whole implication of the utterance is that, before it can be realized, the United States must, by one means or another, undergo a New Reconstruction when such a principle may receive the implementation of life itself.

CHAPTER ELEVEN

STEREOTYPES: THE FRUITS OF "RACE"

AFTER the use of "race" as a political instrument to maintain a restrictive class structure, probably the major consequence of "race" thinking among whites appears in the form of stereotyped ideas of what the Negro is and is not. I am not interested in describing all these misconceptions because I do not wish to produce an encyclopedia, but it can be said that these notions are all traceable to the nation's rise in and with slavery. The ideas of the past, with relation to the Negro, come down to us like pictures on the wall of some decadent old mansion. Most mis-notions were evolved a long time ago when white people who went to church on Sunday and worked their slaves the rest of the week (and sometimes on Sunday, too) had to fashion a set of ideas to convince themselves that what they were doing was all right with nature, man, God, government, and their own souls. Modern racists have not bothered to become original and invent new misconceptions of the Negro. They are willing to go along lazily with the ones which were good enough for their fathers and grandfathers. The only important thing I can say, after close living with the Negro, is that *every one of these ideas is false*.

As a consequence, one of the greatest problems of the Negro is to rid the white mind of its misconceptions concerning what Negroes are and are not. If the Negro can correct the white man's mind and thinking, he can materially change his submerged status. The process of achieving this changed attitude occupies much of the Negro's energies. Negroes eat, sleep, and live the question, "What shall we do about the whites?" One of the proofs of this is how the whole concept of "the Negro question" has been transformed in the last few years into a "white man's problem," which it is. Well, that is one of the gains. Once the issue is over in the white man's lot where it belongs, where it has to be hashed out or thrashed out, some of the battle is won. What has happened in the recent period, with the upswing of Negro rights, is that the battleground is no longer solely in the Negro's front yard—his press, church, cultural, personal, and social life; but in the white man's front yard as well—in the legislatures, the white churches, white cultural areas.

What is involved in this process, in addition to fundamental economic changes, is an educational process, or more correctly, a re-educational process. If the average white man believes that most or all Negroes can sing, which is a misconception, then something has to be said or done to clear up the confusion. White folks are very fond of saying, "They've got rhythm." In fact, I've heard many whites discuss the Negro group and all that they could say for any or all Negroes was, "They've got rhythm." Throughout the South, and perhaps widely in the North, too, there is a dangerous and fatal notion that the average Negro is "childlike," or "simple." John Robert Powers, the beauty authority, phrased it for me this way, "I think as far as the colored are concerned, they have a wonderful, simple, and interesting philosophy."

The myth of the Negro's sense of humor is one of the most mistaken. From the Negro's viewpoint this stereotype is itself most laughable. Some whites believe that the Negro just isn't or can't be a thoughtful person or serious. Others are naive enough to believe that the Negro is innately such an ingenuous sort that he just laughs off his segregated status unconcernedly. Others form their impression of Negro "lightheartedness" from radio and movie comics like "Rochester," passing judgment on all Negroes on the basis of such a very untypical and even unique individual. Negroes daily discuss these twisted reactions of white people. When they relate their experiences with the Jim Crow pattern and the confusion or uncertainty of white Americans, or the unusual contradictions that often develop, I have found them to possess a superb sense of irony. This irony has assumed the proportion of an aesthetic value of great importance to the Negro; it is a stoic thing that I have never encountered among my white friends because there is no especial need for them to possess it. It is irony on a philosophic level. It is a safety valve, a capacity to laugh, but to laugh at the split personality of the white world. It is a laugh that contains a huge criticism and indictment at the same time that it conveys a literal Jim Crow twist. This capacity for having "the last laugh" has enabled Negroes "to bend, instead of to break," as someone put it to me, and it has enabled them to keep their morale alive at moments when the odds would seem insuperable.

Tallulah Bankhead, Alabama-bred, is very convinced of the rhythm which Negroes have. She doesn't say just certain Negroes, but simply Negroes. I had a row with Miss Bankhead over these points. Interviewing her for the *Defender*, at her summer home in Bedford Hills, I was a little chagrined to hear her say that not only were Negroes gay, and not only did they have rhythm, but also that they were childlike. Coming from a traveled and, as I supposed, cosmopolitan person I was a little taken aback. It was especially surprising because I was aware she had known Negroes and been associated with them for many years. Her name has often appeared on liberal and interracial committees.

It is very easy for whites to generalize about Negroes and to want to believe generalities about the Negro. As an example, John Chapman, reviewing the play *Jeb* in the New York *Daily News*, observed, "Negroes must be born actors, for always there is the right man or the right woman for the right part." This belongs to the same type of reasoning which insists that Negroes are born to gaiety, good humor, and don't give a damn about anything tomorrow if they have something to eat today. It happened that the character Chapman was praising for his acting, Ossie Davis, had struggled for three months in hard, heavy rehearsals to perfect himself for the role in that play. He wasn't born for that role, or for any role; in fact, he never expected to be an actor, but trained to be a writer.

As a result of what whites do to the Negro psychology by trying to "type" Negroes, by trying to make them esoteric, primitive, brutal, cowardly, comical, loving, or anything else exotic or "different," individual Negroes in the artistic world have tried to live up to these notions as a means of making a livelihood. Probably the most famous character of this sort was Stephen Fetchit, who, in Hollywood, played dumb-comic-lazy-man roles, created a great laugh at the expense of thirteen million Negroes, made a fortune for himself, and caused white folks to think that Negroes were a scared, shuffling, mumbling lot. Another actress, Hattie McDaniels, made the "mammy" role so famous in Hollywood that she won an Academy Award. The truth, if one is looking for an "average" Negro woman, is more likely to be found in the hardworking mother who helps her husband support the family.

The first time I became aware of how deeply imbedded these figments of the white imagination are in American minds was at a house party in a Fifth Avenue hotel a number of years ago where some literary lights, liberals, and politicos were meeting to raise money for sharecroppers.

The hostess, a very charming white woman of about thirty-eight, was leaning over one side of a grand piano; a Negro friend of mine, Lorenzo Greene, and I were leaning over the other side, and we were engaged in a conversation about Negro and white reactions. Greene, the author of *The Negro in Colonial New England,* is a very scholarly type; and he was in his most reserved and pedantic mood at the time. He and the hostess were discussing the question of Negroes and music.

"My, your people have such wonderful voices," said the hostess.

Greene looked at me with a glance of bedevilment that I have grown used to.

"Do they?" he asked.

"But of course they do," she went on, full of charm. "You *know* they do," and I feared she was going to chuck him under the chin.

"I don't think they can sing especially," he protested mildly.

She insisted.

"But *I* can't sing a note," he pointed out.

There were a few seconds of silence.

"What? You can't sing a note? Really?" She was nonplussed. Her blue eyes were round with disbelief.

"Not a note." The ordinarily sedate professor was adamant. Then, a little irritated, he emphasized, "Not a *goddamned* note, Mrs. H."

Our hostess stopped in her vocal tracks. She looked from Greene to me as if she had been hurt, perhaps insulted. Greene tried to explain.

"Really, Mrs. H, Negroes can't all sing. I know very few of them, in fact, who can sing. When they sing well enough they get up in public and sing, and they're the ones who can sing, but the rest of us can't sing."

Somebody was serving cookies and Mrs. H grabbed the plate and started passing it around herself.

With the passage of a few years, and with a combination of exploration in history and Harlem, I found out why this notion persists. It is an idea that is so deep rooted that I don't know whether my experience and explanation is going to aid any in dispelling it, but I shall try.

One has to look to history for the answer to this, as for the answer to most issues surrounding Negro-white inter-attitudes.

It goes way back to chattel slavery, to the time when Negroes worked as fieldhands on the cotton and rice plantations. It returns to the time when the black people were literally in chains, when work from sunrise to sunset was the rule. As someone once expressed it to me, "Although the Negro's lot is essentially tragic, and although the Negro's essential position as a member of a caste is a tragic one, you can't be tragic all the time—and live." We can verify that today, for, in our period, stories are told of group singing even in concentration camps. Group or individual singing on a plantation was one of the few outlets for the emotions. It was also one of the few recourses allowed the Negro. A singing slave perfectly fitted the specifications of the slavemaster. A man who will slave and sing at the same time may be more contented, may at least *seem* more contented. He would, it was thought, be less apt to be troublesome or cause trouble. I have seen early advertisements of slaves for sale which mentioned, "This slave sings." Negroes who would sing or chant as they tilled the soil were sought for by masters more than others. This was because the slavemaster was interested, not in the music, but solely in having a "satisfied" or a non-rebellious worker, and theoretically, a slave who sang was such a worker. Some overseers drove their slaves to sing by the use of whips. This reveals how terribly much they wanted slaves to accept slavery and be happy about it, too. Histories describe how slaves, working on barges, or grouped together in fields or mills, would break out in song. In the sugar plantations of the West Indies slave singing was cultivated by the overseers who could get unified work out of a row of slaves singing as they labored. It was in this type of labor, performed to the demanded routine of singing, that not only created actual singers very often, but gave rise to the misconception that all Negroes could sing anyway. The singing slave was not necessarily a happy one.

Song was used liberally as a means of communication in escaping to the North. At that time the tradition established by the whites was used against them, and the same tradition is still used by Negroes to advance themselves and gain benefits from a hostile white society. Song, probably never an *organic* characteristic of the Negro any more than of any people, has been acquired, used, de-

135]

veloped as a lever. It has now reached such a stage of perfection as a weapon, that it is also an art.

One night, walking along upper Broadway, I saw a crowd of people gathered around a small Negro boy who was staging a ventriloquist act. He sat on a box, and had on his knee a colored Charlie McCarthy. It looked very cute to the passers-by and they gathered around, watched, and tossed coins.

Actually the boy had no ventriloquist talent at all. When his Charlie McCarthy talked, the boy himself talked pretty audibly; but the whole scene *looked* clever. What the boy had was a good social and business sense. He knew that the Negro has a tradition as an entertainer; he had learned that a Negro who can entertain may sometimes cross the bars, may get an audience. He was working on the *tradition,* not his talent. And people tossed him coins too, not because of his talent, which held nobody for very long, but because the tradition of expecting a Negro to entertain was here being re-enacted for them, and the white people responded as a patronizing class of people is supposed to respond.

Probably the best example I know of this situation, one that can be put to a test every Wednesday night—by those who live in or near New York—is to listen in to the amateur hour that is put on at the Apollo Theatre in Harlem over station WMCA. Those who wish to make an anthropological experiment of their own may measure what I have stated here against the evidence of their own ears and judgment. On that night one will hear about ten or fifteen young people, Negroes, of both sexes, get up before the microphone and sing. The fact that their voices are already "good enough" so that they are willing to get up before a critical audience presumably sets them apart from the average Negro as having something to offer. One or two voices at most, out of the whole group, will have any talent at all. The others are hooted off the stage in a very brutal way . . . someone called "Puerto Rico," who operates a fire siren, turns it on whenever a voice doesn't show up well or when he gets the signal from the audience.

[136

STEREOTYPES: THE FRUITS OF "RACE"

First, this amateur hour proves that not all Negroes can sing; second, it proves that a great many of them, who are willing to get up before a crowded theatre, sing badly; third, it proves that anyone who does get the applause that means he is acceptable as a singer, still has to struggle before he or she can ever really get anywhere as a professional. Finally, the number of amateurs who have developed and amounted to anything in the course of this institution, which has been going on for decades, is less than the fingers of one hand.

My curiosity took me a little deeper into this question.

I decided to secure from the lips of a typical struggling singer an opinion on the matter. I sought out Carol Brice, a young Negro woman who possesses a contralto voice that has been highly praised. She is now at "mid-passage" in her career; she is on her way up. Interviewing her for my paper, I wanted to know whether she was born with her fine voice, whether singing was natural to her, and whether she believed singing was natural to most or all Negroes. She suggested that in her particular case she might have inherited some vocal ability from her mother and her father, both of whom were active in church and college singing, and both of whom had pretty good voices. But she pointed out that singing was something she had to *win,* that excellence was something she was struggling for. "My struggle has not been with race, but with music," she explained. Then she told me how she had cultivated her voice for many years, during her high-school days, in her years at the Juilliard Graduate School of Music, and with incessant private instruction. She had had to study languages, she had sung in church choirs; and even having a child, she thought, had helped her voice. More, she could feel her talent growing, but only as she studied, trained, struggled. She pointed out that many Negroes who may have a certain amount of vocal ability never emerge as singers perhaps because they do not understand that a great voice has to be won and mastered.

No, the average Negro cannot just walk up on the platform and

137]

give you a rendition of either "Carmen" or "Old Man River." Most of the great Negro singers have emerged in their thirties after long fights with music, with the music industry, and sometimes with "racial" handicaps.

But the reason why Negroes are found so often in the music world is because slavery itself produced the tradition that admits Negroes to the world of song: the tradition that wants them to sing, lets them in when they can sing well . . . pays them when they put on a feeble ventriloquist act, too. Negroes have utilized the world of art and the sphere of music, and it is right that they have walked up this avenue, for most others have been closed to them. Even now they cannot get into the Metropolitan Opera Company, and as a consequence they have their own National Negro Opera Company. If a Negro can make a living singing, if a hostile white economic and commercial world will cock its ear toward the Negro when he sings, it is natural that a disproportionate number will attempt to get economic security through this means. Let it go on so, too, but it is wise for white Americans to broaden their conceptions so as to cease thinking in narrow terms of the abilities of the Negro. We learned in World War II that the Negro could run any kind of a machine that a white man could run; that Negroes worked, in a scientific capacity, on the atom-bomb project.

Negroes, like the rest of the reasoning creatures of the world, are the same human beings, or animals, whichever one chooses. If we bury our heads in the sand and limit them to "They can sing," and forget that they can also run machines and airplanes, we are most obviously ostriches.

Very much the same thing applies to the Negro and the "They've got rhythm" idea. This, too, traces back to slavery, back to the galley ship that brought the Negro to the West Indies from Africa.

About three centuries ago when slave traders started running the Middle Passage route from Africa to the West Indies, with their slave captives, it was deathly close and hot on board, and the

STEREOTYPES: THE FRUITS OF "RACE"

Africans died as rapidly as occupants of a concentration camp. One of the devices of the ship captains to forestall a too heavy loss of life from suffocation and general suffering was to lash the slaves up on deck and make them dance. They also enjoyed the sight of the Negroes' dancing. The captives knew their own unique African dances, their tribal steps and swings, and they did their stuff. So the first knowledge of white men about what a Negro stood for was in this exhibition of talent, and the slave-runners muttered, "They've got rhythm."

On the plantations where the owners and the overseers had no interest in the black man other than exacting labor power and labor time from his harassed body, they also made the Negroes dance and sing, and the plantation lords uttered the same line, "They've got rhythm."

The white man who enslaved the Negro did not want to believe that his slave had any capacity other than to work and dance and perhaps sing. He encouraged all three. So long as the white man told himself this black was limited, perhaps not even a man, that all he could do was work, and that his only talents were dancing and singing and being gay, he could fashion the concept of a satisfied, childlike being who perfectly suited the purposes of profit.

Three hundred years is a long time for a concept to steep in a people's institutions, and I no longer am surprised when I hear my white friends say, profoundly, as if they knew the Negro, "They've got rhythm."

I try to tell them that the Negro may or may not have rhythm; that in either case it's not vitally significant. I try to tell them that the Negro has capacities, beauties, talents, mentality—everything that everybody else has—if he be given a chance to show his wares.

"They've got rhythm." History has nailed this slogan upon the white mind and heart and soul. After Reconstruction, and after the turn of the nineteenth century, it was still pretty difficult for the mass of Negroes to break into industry, into the sciences and arts. An occasional dancing team appeared on the Keith vaudeville circuit; the old "They've got rhythm" routine deepened itself in the American concept of what the Negro was. In our own time there is even a Negro group calling itself "The Rhythm Boys," actually trading on this tradition; I don't exactly blame them, if they can make some headway as a result.

But I've watched thousands of Negroes as they move along Harlem's streets, and they walk like men and women, not like swaying willows, even if white America tries to tell itself that the Negro moves with some exotic rhythm. Colored people come into my office all day long. They enter and sit here and talk with me and leave with the same grace, or lack of it, as white people: no more. I am convinced, too, that if anthropologists examined this question they would find that the black man has no more "rhythm" than any other people. They would be more likely to find an historical explanation of it in our socio-economic past, as I have suggested.

I am not trying to take "rhythm" away from the Negro if the Negro has got it, and if it does him any good. My objection is that white America very mistakenly believes that this "primitivism" is often the be-all and end-all of the Negro. My objection is that whites misinform themselves with an exotic conception of their fellow Americans by that sage, serious-faced observation, "The Negro has got rhythm."

This kind of "knowledge" of Negroes exists in place of real information about them.

Recently I talked with an old Negro scholar, Charles C. Seifert, who lives in Harlem. He has studied African, American, and world history for forty years and he has a fund of knowledge. His general philosophic thesis is that the modern industrial, technological, Western-Christian world is a flowering of elementary principles in industrial, agricultural, moral, and economic ways of life originated in Africa. In his intense pro-African view he is inclined to claim every conceivable virtue for the person born with black skin. I happen to agree with him that a great deal in modern culture does stem from pre-Christian, African civilizations, but Seifert's tendency to claim essential superiority for the Negro is as wrong for him as Representative Rankin's claim of organic white superiority is wrong for Rankin. Seifert believes that the Negro has, as a physical property, more rhythm than the white.

He offered an illustration of the black man's superior rhythmic faculties. He described how, in the West Indies, on the sugar plantations, the overseers would work their slaves in unison. The overseer or a slave hortator would sing out some slogan such as "Blow, blow, blow the man down." As he said "down" fifty or a hundred slaves would come down with their spades; this performance would be repeated, over and over, in unison and in rhythm. The effect was to convey the sight of a mass of men operating in rhythm, and they were able to perform this way because they had a natural propensity to move gracefully and together.

I believe Professor Seifert's point was a little labored, and his illustration not very conclusive. I think white men slaving in a cotton, tobacco, or rice field, could at the threat of a whiplash very probably develop the same kind of unified motion.

Now why was Professor Seifert interested in contending that Negroes do have more rhythm than whites? Simply because he, like most Negroes, is part of a great fight to convince white Americans that Negroes are as good as whites. One way to do this is to claim that Negroes are better, and therefore many Negroes are willing to use music, rhythm, Joe Louis, Paul Robeson, George Washington Carver, Richard Wright, or anyone else or anything else of whose superiority white men are already partially convinced, if it will help.

After Joe Louis became world's heavyweight champion, the prize ring as a means of advance for Negroes drew scores of young Negro men into its orbit. There was a more or less conscious attempt to prove that Negroes can get into the ring and fight.

I saw a sorry example of that.

A twenty-nine-year-old Negro, father of two children, came into my office one day and asked my assistance in helping him collect sixty dollars owed to him, he said, by the Rhode Island State Boxing Commission for a fight he had just had in Providence, for which he was not paid. He explained he had been knocked out in the first round. The fight fans believed he had laid down and booed him, and he was not paid. Actually he had been knocked out, fairly and squarely, because he didn't know much about fighting. He explained to me he was a little tired too because he had fought somebody else the day before; he had lasted three rounds in that fight to earn fifteen dollars before being knocked out.

"How long have you been fighting?" I asked.

"About two years."

"Did you ever win a fight?"

He dropped his eyes, admitted he hadn't; said he had fought forty fights.

"Is this the only way you can make a living?"

"Well, I get some income that way. I can get booked."

"You started fighting pretty late, didn't you?"

"Yes."

I had the feeling he would get punch-drunk before long if he continued to take whippings. Here was a man who kept on in the boxing game with very little ability; he was working on the new-grown tradition of the Negro as a prize fighter.

I have seen small boys boxing in the streets of Harlem, training, practicing, learning, in the hope one day of entering an occupational arena opened to the Negro. The prize ring is in the air, in Harlem, like rhythm and music, and I should not be surprised, if Joe Louis wins more fights, were the theory to be advanced in the white world, and to some extent accepted in the Negro world, that all Negroes under any and all circumstances are better with their mitts than white people.

Thus, under my eyes, I have seen the process by which a stereotype threatens to develop. White America insists on generalizing from the individual Negro to the whole group, persists in viewing the people of color as different, special, alien, primitive. Because a writer once created a character named Uncle Tom, millions of whites contend that Negroes are meek, submissive, quiet, loving, saintly, and know how to stay "in their place." Another writer projects a character like Bigger Thomas, and promptly thousands of whites conceive of the Negro, in his main potential, as brutal, as a rapist, as animalistic. All of these mis-notions fit into handy compartments in the minds of Americans who want the Negro to be apart from white America, apart from the mainstream of national life.

Currently there is a great ferment among Negroes to re-educate their misdirected white brothers and sisters into understanding of the simple fact that Negroes are as fallible and as great, as kind and as hating, as noble and ignoble as the rest of humanity. If the Negro has seemed to emerge with special emphases and special qualities for periods of time, it is because he has been subject to inordinate pressures which have propelled him and molded him in such ways that he has appeared to have propensities that others do not have.

As a Negro might state it, "The white American is sick with a kind of social delirium tremens and sees all kinds of strange things where there are really only harassed human beings."

CHAPTER TWELVE

SEMANTICS, ROMANTICS, AND LEGAL-ANTICS

"Words spoken or written are with money the two great powers that there are."

—MBONU OJIKE in *My Africa*

A WHITE Southerner walked onto the campus of a Negro college in the South. He wore a large broad-rimmed hat and loose, wrinkled trousers; his white shirt flopped about at his waist a little sloppily. There was a holster around his middle and a gun in the holster. He was chewing tobacco, and spitting occasionally as he walked. He was blue-eyed and red-necked and his thick drawl filled out the picture of what my Negro informant called "a typical cracker."

The white man stopped a Negro on the campus and asked, "Say here, you know where I kin find a nigger named Williams?"

"You mean Professor Williams?"

"Yah, where kin I find that nigger?"

The white man was directed to a certain building, and, leaving some kind of a grunt for thanks, went on.

Finally he came to the door of Professor Williams.

"Are you nigger Williams?"

"I am Professor Williams," corrected the head of the department of philosophy. "What can I do for you?"

" 'Taint what you can do for me. I jest want to talk to you."

The professor noticed the gun in the holster, nervously laid aside his papers, cleared his throat, and started listening.

"You got a gal in yore class named Emmy Lou Jones?"

"Why, yes," said Professor Williams, thinking of a pretty brown-skinned girl who didn't respond to instruction in philosophy so well.

"Well, you the nigger thet flunked her last week?"

"Well, now you mention it, I believe she didn't get passing marks. I'm afraid Emmy Lou . . ."

"You haint afraid o' the right thing," interrupted the white man. "You better be afraid o' this here," and he laid his gun on top of the professor's papers.

"What's the . . . er, ah . . . what's the tr—?"

"Trouble is you better change them there marks o' hern."

"Well, I'll do whatever I can to . . ."

"You'll change them there marks o' Emmy Lou's or you haint ever a-goin' to make no more marks," and the white man twirled the revolver around on the papers.

The professor promised to pass Emmy Lou right away.

The white man spat some tobacco juice into the professor's wastebasket, picked up his gun, and turned about. He stopped at the door just long enough to say, somewhat as an afterthought, "That gal's my daughter, see?"

Yet I have no doubt that if anyone were to ask that same white father of a Negro girl whether he advocated marriage of Negro and white, he would probably take the gun out of his holster and, this time, shoot.

The story got around, and an acquaintance of mine, a white lecturer, once had occasion to repeat it to a group of women I shall call the "Ladies' Aid Society." He had recited the story in evidence of the fact that in reality there is no issue about advocating sex relations between Negro and white. Like the weather, it is here all the time, he pointed out, and the most that anyone can do is express an opinion about it—particularly in view of the fact that there is the blood of so-called whites in eight million so-called Negro Americans.

When my friend had finished relating the episode and there had been some general laughter, and after he had given an historical picture of marriage relations between the two groups, a matronly and highly respectable-looking woman arose to ask a question. My friend told me he could sense her outrage twenty yards away. "Young man," she demanded, "I will mince no words. I want to know how you stand on one fundamental matter, since you seem so tolerant of the idea of our mingling with these people. Would you yourself go to sleep with a Negro woman?"

There was a ripple of surprise at the directness of her question, and then a hush over the audience of about one hundred women when, mincing no words, my friend replied, "Madame, I would go to bed with a Negro woman, but I'll be damned if I'd go to sleep."

Whether or not he made the proper reply is beside the point. Perhaps she didn't ask the proper question. Question and answer were both pretty personal, and it had the effect then of causing a general fit of hysterical laughter.

For an anticlimax, after the flurry subsided, another woman arose, fully as irate as the first, and tucking in her bosom, directed this demand at the lecturer:

"Mr. R, this may seem like a very personal question to ask of you also, but will you please tell us— What does your own family think of you?"

My friend told me that he had been waiting for that one for ten years and had the answer all ready and polished. "Madame, I am afraid I am the black sheep in the family."

The question of marriage of Negro and white is one that is most intimately related to the business of "race." Society has evolved a number of expensive words to describe the impossibility of the

[146

East meeting the West, and black meeting white. Such words as *amalgamation, intermarriage,* and *miscegenation* are a few of the offenders intended to frighten people into staying within their own national, religious, and ethnic provinces. Each of these terms suggests insurmountable walls, forbidden fruit, sin, crime, and revolt. Webster's *Dictionary* of 1883 defined the term *miscegenation* as "a recent and ill-formed word." It may have originated in the nineteenth century, and it grew up out of the labyrinthine Southern black codes seeking to prevent union of white and Negro. Actually a legal term bearing a criminal onus, the word has often been used to describe "violation of racial purity." The word is a semantic and legal consequence of the political-economic history I have been citing. At the founding of the country there was no such word, for separation of people on a color basis was not yet clearly evolved. The gradual creation of the social malpractice of segregation brought the term *miscegenation* into being in its legal definition as "a mixing of races; amalgamation." The legal term then passed into everyday use, to help foster and deepen the forbidden nature of legal marriage between the color groups. It became accepted conceptually in many states as part of "the way of life."

Professor Albert Einstein, who is as wise in living as he is in the sphere of science, split the miscegenation atom this way, "I cannot believe that animals who can have children together can be very profoundly different from each other."

One of the most interesting observations on "amalgamation" ever made to me was that of Freda Kirchwey, the editor of *The Nation.* "Brazil points a great meaning for America," said Miss Kirchwey, who has lived there. "They have got something we haven't got. That is the attitude between peoples. Color plays none of the role that it does here. There is an easy-going feeling among people so far as color and origins are concerned. And I do not know but that if one had to choose between the social level of Brazil, this feeling of brotherhood among colors and nationalities, and our own industrial order with its frictions and gulfs, I might choose the Brazilian—even with its other backwardness. For here is one of the fundamental problems of human understanding, and Brazil, in this respect, is way ahead of us."

A Brazilian visiting in Harlem once confirmed this for me in a curious way. Some Negro acquaintances and I started questioning him about "what he was." This is an old familiar pattern here, of course. We want to know whether a man is British or French, black or white, Protestant or Catholic. We often pry until we find out these things. In our country there are still whirlpools of the past moving in the mainstream. There are the "Little Italys," the black ghettos, the Irish neighborhoods. There is everywhere a melting-pot tendency, but as yet no melted pot. Anyway, the Brazilian, in whose features and coloring one could see Europe, Africa, and the Indians of South America, shrugged his shoulders and said: "I don't know what you mean. I feel like a Brazilian."

Thus we have the contradiction, in the Western Hemisphere, of the backward, feudal, and sometimes semi-dictatorship countries in the lands to the south being far advanced in an understanding of the elementary humanity of all peoples. Brazil is the living editorial which tells us the lie of "race." That country, if it does not yet reflect the economy of "The Century of the Common Man," may, however, be ahead of the rest of the world and already living in "The Century of the Non-ethnic Man." And this is largely because one leader, Simon Bolivar, the George Washington of South America, saw that there could be no harmony on that continent unless the Latins, Indians, and Negroes amalgamated. He therefore decreed that the peoples unite. The story is generally accepted that he insisted upon his daughters marrying Negroes to symbolize and project this philosophy.

To those who ask about advocacy of marriage or other social relations between the groups, the action of Bolivar and the results of his position are already part of the world's progressive history. But just as Brazil's integrated sociological character was determined

[148

from the top, so too, in America, has segregation been decreed from the top.

It was 1622 when the first supremacist-minded legislature in America, then in Virginia, established a fine for fornication between Negro and white. Apparently white and Negro servants, neither of whom had been in the country more than a few years, had no serious objections to social relations. The royal corporations of Britain and Holland which settled America at that time ruled on an aristocratic-feudal basis. There were only two classes. There were at one extreme the aristocratic pioneers who ran the colonies, and at the other the black and white servants or slaves. These laborers lived together on their plane as the aristocrats lived by themselves on theirs. Fraternization of black and white at that time, before any system of segregation had developed, found both groups generally unprejudiced about each other. Working together daily, perhaps slaving together, they had their class and economic condition in common, and they associated and sought common understanding.

For the first one hundred years of Virginia's history, as the records of its courts prove, association between white and Negro toilers was so extensive that millions of light-colored Negroes of today can trace their white inheritance back to that period.

It was necessary for Virginia lawmakers to pound away at restrictive legislation year after year for three hundred years to *create* attitudes of superiority. Consult a book called *The Black Laws of Virginia,* by June Purcell Guild, and glance at the enormous file of laws passed annually from the colonial period right through to the present. One chapter alone, "The Struggle for Racial Integrity," proves that substantial numbers of whites constantly rejected the state's position. Life repudiated the lawmakers and forced them repeatedly to make war on the marriage of the two peoples. In spite of fines, physical punishments, long jail terms, lynchings, lashings, rulings, and policing, the people of Virginia,

149]

white and Negro, following a more natural law than any that could be enacted by the officialdom, defied the decrees and ordinances, and, in practice, advocated and carried on social relations. Where marriage was illegalized, white men resorted to concubinage. In fact, in that respect, most Southern states have grown to sanction this, which is social treatment of the Negro woman on a basis of inequality.

Recently a young Unitarian minister, the Reverend Frank Glenn White, whose parish was in Norfolk, Virginia, decided to break through the wall of prejudice in that community in a very definite way. His preachments for interracial harmony aroused the wrath of the church elders and they asked him to resign. Meantime he was keeping company with Miss Anne Anderson, a young Negro woman who was separated from her husband. Reverend White, who wanted to marry her and set up an interracial church, knew they wouldn't be able to remain in Virginia. When the couple came to my office I put them in touch with the Reverend Claude Williams, founder of the People's Institute of Applied Religion, and he placed them in charge of the Institute's work in New York. The couple planned to symbolize the interracial church and at the same time rebuke the church nationally for its policy of segregation by having a large public wedding at Congressman Adam C. Powell's church in Harlem. I splashed the story in my paper and the event became big news in the Negro press; the white dailies and news services suppressed it. Virginia, however—and this is the point of the story—always ready for a fight against people in love if they are of different color, discovered a technicality. Anne Anderson believed she was divorced, and so did her husband. Virginians, whose marriage law moves as feudally as their law for Negroes, threatened to arrest her for bigamy. The marriage was naturally called off until the divorce should be final. What was significant was not that the state officialdom of Virginia cares whether its Negroes are married, single, divorced, or dead, but that it could not tolerate the interracial symbolization of this particular

[150

event. So the Virginians moved swiftly to invoke their ancient and perennial prerogative of keeping black and white separated, as introduced by the martial law of the Virginia Company three hundred and twenty years before. Reverend White and Miss Anderson went ahead with their interracial work in New York anyway.

Does this mean Negroes necessarily want to marry whites? Not by a long shot. The most interesting repercussions of the White-Anderson news stories my paper carried were the protests of numerous Negroes. I had expected this, for the ideas of white supremacy have created the nationalist-racial reactions which drive many Negroes into a corresponding shell of group feeling. The interracial marriages that have taken place so far in America have been fraught with great hardship. The social pressures against such couples in the Negro and white worlds have been oppressive. Mixed couples have had to live virtually underground. What Reverend White and Miss Anderson wanted to do was to break this issue out into the light of day everywhere, to bring interracial marriages out from underground, to make it easier for other such couples to live openly, publicly, legally, like human beings, as a man and woman ought to be able to live, for the world to see and respect.

The White-Anderson episode was one more confirmation of the contention that no matter what state or federal law may have ruled in the past, or may be ruling at present, about association between Negro and white, the people make their own law when it is necessary. Charles S. Magnum, Jr. in his authoritative *Legal Status of the Negro* confirms this when he cites Louisiana as a state where there has been so much infusion of Negro blood in the white citizenry "that a marriage license would be refused only in cases where the admixture is evident from the appearance or other characteristics of the party making the application." In that state the marriage of white persons to individuals with only a slight admixture of Negro blood is usually attacked only by those interested in the succession to property.

I have heard many very naive people express incredulity when I point out that the Negro often uses the term "fascism" to describe his social experience in America. When we don't wear a tight shoe it can't hurt. Look how segregation in Mississippi slops over into the arena of a free press: that state as recently as 1930 enacted a law punishing anybody for publishing, printing, or circulating any literature in favor of or urging interracial marriage or social equality. We have laws on the books in the United States, which the average citizen doesn't know about, which rule against about three-fifths of the world's population. Fifteen Far Western states directly or by implication forbid marriage between Caucasians and Chinese; ten states prevent whites and Malays from marriage; five bar unions of whites and Indians; Louisiana and Oklahoma prevent Indians and Negroes from marriage; Maryland rules out union of Malays and Negroes; Georgia and Virginia forbid Asiatic Indians and whites from marrying. In one Alabama case, according to Magnum, "It was said that the fact that a dark-skinned individual comes from Sicily is not conclusive evidence that he or she is wholly white. . . . The meaning of the term 'Creole' in any given bit of testimony is a question to be decided by the jury under proper instruction from the court. The term is subject to divers interpretations, one designating the French-speaking inhabitants of Louisiana and the other nearby states, another indicating a people of the same kind with a slight admixture of Negro blood."

The question needs to be asked: Is the dominant group really interested in the color or ethnology of a people or is it interested simply in maintaining economic supremacy?

An ordinance passed in Fort Worth, Texas, in 1915, very candidly admits the economic irresponsibility behind this segregative legislation. The ordinance says it is unlawful for Negroes and whites to have sexual intercourse within the city limits. What is the purpose of this? The purpose is so that white men may escape economic responsibility for relations with Negro women.

In most of the so-called miscegenation cases before state and federal courts the determining issues have revolved around such questions as the right to custody of children by "mixed" marriages, the right to inherit or share in property, the responsibility toward support by white fathers of children by colored women, and kindred situations. That the courts have usually ruled against the Negro proves only that the courts have sought to deny the people of color property rights and economic security. This property approach to the Negro has not only resulted in the denial to him of his economic rights, but it has projected the whole issue of Negro-white relations into the arena of property rights rather than human rights. As long as American courts are able to rob the Fourteenth Amendment of the human equation intended by its authors, as long as most issues are reduced to their cash value, the Negro will be the victim rather than the beneficiary of the principal amendment that came out of the Civil War.

The United States Supreme Court sustains such laws and the legislatures making them as not violating the guarantees of the Fourteenth Amendment. In the Missouri case of *State versus Jackson*, in 1883, it was said that the privileges and immunities of federal citizenship guaranteed by the amendment did not include the right to marry outside of one's own race. What this means is that a large number of state legislatures supported by the highest court of the land undertake to tell Americans whom they may marry and whom they may not. In Germany this policy was called part of the totalitarian setup; over here we call it part of the democratic system.

One could quote endlessly from American law to show how the states have had to be perennially aggressive in building up, protecting, and maintaining the man-made idea of segregation. The great simple and single truth that unfolds from this realization is that since law, based on economic need for a source of cheap labor, has manufactured the caste system, law can, in a great measure, unmake it. Those who say one cannot legislate discrimination and prejudice out of existence are in some cases honestly mistaken, while others, who know better, deliberately lie. "Education" is a vague concept indeed if it does not have the force of the state behind it. Carey McWilliams is right when he contends "Legislation is education." This means that the great re-educational process which America must undergo is very largely a re-legislative process.

What is important for people to understand when asked whether they advocate intermarriage, is that the officialdom of so many American states, supported by the Supreme Court, has no hesitation about advocating segregation. It would be better to advocate the marriage of people of any color, than to advocate the repression and suppression of any people. The right to marry should be an individual choice, a matter of preference and taste, but in the United States the individual's right to choose is abridged. This means that the right of millions of whites to their free choice is estopped just as much as the right of Negroes. Finally, when the lawmaking bodies of the land take such a consistent stand in advocacy of oppressive measures, can the people fail to advocate opposite measures?

CHAPTER THIRTEEN

THE PRINCIPLE OF INTEGRATION

Tʜɪs friend was born in a small town in the West. His was the only Negro family in the community; and from boyhood he was aware of his color difference. He was treated politely by everyone, but he knew that in the privacy of the provincial homes he and his parents were discussed as a special, local phenomenon. He was under a certain strain to be good, to be right, to excel, to be exemplary; and he became the high school's valedictorian, champion athlete, and young man of great promise.

When graduation day arrived and the senior prom was in the offing, the principal called him to the office and said: "George, you are the finest young man in the school. You have walked off with all the honors. You will go far. That is why I know you will understand when I say that I don't think you should go to the senior prom. You will be a wallflower there, and you won't be happy. You know, George, it wouldn't be right for you to dance with our girls. You know that, now, don't you?"

When my friend told me this story, how the crowning hours of his high-school career were scarred by denial of his elementary right to walk among those with whom he had grown up, I could understand his outburst, as, storming about my apartment, he said: "I tell you this white man will go down! This white man is not fit to live! This white man will yet learn that one-and-one-half billions of people are of different skin colorings than he, and these may flood over and drown out the white civilization!"

This is the wrath and the anger of the unintegrated. This is the hate, a hate often made inevitable, of a people forced to reason in terms of color. This may well be the resolve of thousands of Negroes compelled to look with anger, mistrust, suspicion, and even loathing upon a mass of people domineering, indifferent, frequently vicious, rarely fully understanding. I tell the incident of my friend only because it illustrates the underlying principle of Negro American life—*the quest for integration*. One cannot be close to the problem very long without hearing that word. *Integration* is what the Negro has not got. He is on the outside and he wants to be on the inside. He is not allowed to play or live or work as others and he wants to play, live, work as others. He occupies a negative position, and desires the positive. The principle of integration (and its opposite, non-integration) cuts a pattern through the nation just as widespread but far more complex than the transportation system over which trains roll, planes fly, farm wagons crawl, and people walk.

Enter a theatre in a white neighborhood, notice the uniform white faces: the principle is present; or go to a picture show in a Negro quarter, see the solidly black group; the principle is there. Even when one observes mixed groups the principle is still there, albeit moving toward democratic arrangement: yet until there is no longer a Negro-white issue the principle will be with us, no matter where there may be islands of cooperation, association, and understanding.

All day long, year in and year out of the lives of thirteen million, this quest for integration is lived. Negroes pass their relaxed time telling one another stories of their perennial experience in coping with the Jim Crow pattern.

A Negro walks along the street and thirty yards away a white person approaches. The Negro visualizes the word "nigger" passing through the white man's mind. He may be right in seeing it

[156

or he may imagine it, but the consciousness of two worlds within the American "One World" is ever present.

The Negro gets on a bus in the South. He must wait until the white man climbs aboard first; he has to watch what the white man will do from instant to instant and adjust himself to the course the dominant man pursues.

A Negro walks into a building in Birmingham. He sees two elevators, one marked "White," the other "Colored." But on that marked "Colored" he also sees a sign reading, "Out of order," and he has to enter the elevator marked "White." A Negro is running that elevator and white people are entering it. What shall he do? Can he enter the same elevator? He looks over the white people, who simply stare at him. The elevator operator motions to him to step in. But there is the hesitancy, the uncertainty each instant, the dangerous pattern that must be observed, tripped over, skipped around, butted against.

Whites are involved in this pattern each minute of the day too. Certainly this is so in the South and in the urban centers of the North. Thousands of whites also try to cope with the situation, to correct themselves, to do the right thing. Sometimes they stumble over themselves miserably trying to be polite. I recall the well-intentioned industrialist who, preceding me on a speaking program before a Negro group, indicated how free he was from prejudice. He opened his talk this way: "Friends, fellow citizens: One word I never, never use is *nigger*." I imagine in rhetoric or philosophy one might call this a pretzel conception, one that turns in on itself.

There is the pathos of supremacist ideas seeping down into the Negro group and infecting people of color with as much prejudice and confusion as the whites. A prominent figure in the interracial world described an incident which illustrates. He went to an interracial banquet, found his seat, and a colored woman with whom he was acquainted seated herself opposite. The dinner hour had not yet arrived, so he asked if she cared to dance. She declined cordially, and he did not pursue the request for he was not an especially good dancer. But suddenly she said, "Quick, Mr. G, dance with me, please." Mr. G. escorted the lady, a cream-colored woman, onto the floor, started dancing, and asked why she had so abruptly changed her mind. She replied: "Oh, didn't you see who was coming toward us? It was Mr. J. He's so black he frightens me to death."

Riding the ferryboat to the Statue of Liberty one day I was shocked to notice a sign on a lavatory door reading "Colord Crew Only." (It was spelled just that way.) I looked at the sign and then out the window at the statue only a mile or so distant. The name of the boat was the *Francis Scott Key*. I looked around at the crew of whites and Negroes. Then I saw another men's room; it was for whites I supposed, for on the door, in gilt letters, was the word "Gentlemen."

For three days I was embroiled with the captain of that ferryboat and the Baltimore owners of the ferryboat concession before I secured their promise to paint over that sign and allow the Negro crew the far better facilities of the whites. The captain, a North Carolina man, saw the point when I explained that the Jim Crow sign on a boat going to the Statue of Liberty was pretty unendurable. He grinned and said, "Yeh, that's a little too raw, isn't it?" For weeks I spread stories of the incident in the *Defender*. It was a classic illustration of Jim Crow, I felt then, and I still feel so. I went through the red tape of a customs examination and fingerprinting to secure a photograph showing that Jim Crow door with, through a window in the background, Miss Liberty pointing her torch aloft:

> *Give me your tired, your poor,*
> *Your huddled masses yearning to breathe free. . . .*

Although the paradox in that situation was unusually graphic, such discrimination incidents occur all over the land each moment. Negroes and enlightened whites fight these things daily in the

[158

courts, by writing letters of protest, sometimes by defending themselves physically. This perennial protest, this constant process of
"straightening things out" is the struggle for integration. It goes
on, piecemeal, step by step, all over the nation. It is a vast process
of resistance, a wholesale declaration of independence, attempting
to undo what the national economy, legal system, and political
policy have bequeathed to all of us.

People try. Even the most reactionary Southern whites so often
believe they are democratic and liberal. This is one of the greatest
contradictions, too: that the South, where the burden lies heaviest
upon all, is also the stronghold of the party called "Democratic."
Youthful Mark Harris, author of the pro-Negro novel *Trumpet
to the World,* told me what happened just after he had finished
speaking over the Mary Margaret McBride radio hour. A Virginia
woman approached him and, wishing to impress him with her
liberality, explained the kind deed she had performed in a Jim
Crow bus only a few days before. "Just the other day I was on a bus
down home," she said. "I was sitting in the colored section of the
bus. I got up and gave my seat to a colored lady and I went and
sat in *my* section." You might call that a self-portrait of a Virginia
liberal. A moment later, a South Carolina woman tried to convey
to Harris the great democracy of her state. She said, "You know,
in the South we take care of them when they're sick, take soup
down to their cabins and all." But her sixteen-year-old daughter
corrected: "Why, mother, how can you say that? We still talk
about that but you know we haven't done that for three generations." Mother was still living with Jefferson Davis.

Confusion, uncertainty, darkness, illiberal liberalism, white
blackness and black whiteness. Said Milton, "Man's inhumanity to
man makes countless thousands mourn." And perhaps the crepe
hangs blackest on white America.

I chanced to be witness to a most significant integration experiment in the summer of 1944 when, as a newspaperman, I covered

159]

an interracial project initiated in northern Vermont by A. Ritchie Low, a minister of the town of Johnson. Reverend Low visited Congressman Powell in Harlem, and hit upon the idea of inviting children of Powell's parish to come and visit the farmers of Vermont for a few weeks. Low extended the invitation, then went back to Vermont and asked for volunteers from the people in the northern part of the state to put up the youngsters. The Vermonters responded heartily, so one hot summer's day a contingent of eighty youngsters aged eight to twelve boarded a train for Vermont, and, at Burlington, were met by people who came in autos from various towns. The children were spread out, one or two to a town, through some eighteen counties.

For about three days I was stationed in Johnson, where the project centered, and I went from one farmhouse to another to see how the visitors were being entertained.

Once I was seated in an automobile with five or six native Vermont children, waiting for a Negro girl to come out of a school. A seven-year-old boy impatiently said, "I wish that little nigger girl would hurry up." The others pounced upon him, not with their hands, but with sharp admonitions never to use that word again. I was surprised at the good manners and good training and good sense of these youngsters, none more than ten. They had been told about what was right and what was wrong. They were doing their best and their best was good.

I perceived in this little incident how America was already struggling to change its approach; how simple it would be for my America to teach understanding if it set out to do so everywhere as the little town of Johnson was doing. This was happening in what New Yorkers and Chicagoans might derisively call "the backwoods." Johnson, town of only eighteen hundred people, was leading the nation in respect of democracy.

One old lady who had no family of her own wept bitterly when it was time for the little eight-year-old Negro girl who stayed with her to go back to New York. I watched white and Negro boys

and girls playing together in amity, equality, and fine understanding day after day. The Harlem kids taught the farm children the
games of the city's streets, and the farm kids taught their big-city
friends the secrets of the farm and the maple-treed forestland. But
the important thing was not that the Harlem kids had contact with
nature and the out-of-doors, good as that was for them. I asked
young Tom Wills of Harlem what, during his stay, had impressed
him most, what had meant more than anything else to him, and he
thought an instant and he said, "Playing with the boy next door."
It was the perfect answer.

The A. Ritchie Low movement spread to other states the following year, and it is now a national project of churches and interracial
groups in many areas.

Like Christopher Columbus who proved that the world was
round; like the economic thinkers who, after thousands of years of
philosophy, discovered the simple fact that the struggle for food,
clothing, and shelter is the major determinant and drive in society;
so A. Ritchie Low had discovered a great truth in a simple act.
He had learned that the situation which is opposite to segregation
is *association*. He had discovered that the thing to do when people
do not understand each other is to bring them together. Call this
Christianity, or integration, or Americanism, or what you will, yet
it was a symptom of the changing of the times, and when I returned to New York I had the feeling that color thinking was in
some degree on the wane.

The only time I ever participated in the life of an institution
practicing full integration was in the early 1930's, when I found
a curiously "pure" equality in New York's biggest flophouse. I was
without a place to sleep one night, penniless, and tired. Not having
the desire to barge in on any of my acquaintances, and hoping
I could ride out this squall on my own, I headed for the Municipal
Lodging House on East 25th Street.

It was evening. Twilight settled over the lower East Side like a woman covering her homely face with a shawl, as I, a little uncertain, rounded the corner that led to the "lodging house." The sidewalks were filthy with debris, the disinherited moved wearily through the streets.

It was not until I had registered—one has to give quite a bit of one's pedigree to get in there—and sat down at a long table where something called stew was being served, that I noticed the tremendously polyglot nature of the guests of the city. About one-fourth of the diners were Negro. The others were everything else that America alone can get together under one roof.

We sat beside each other, mixed as the stew itself, and no man looked askance at another for his color and possible national origin. The atmosphere was so much like a jail, sardine box, military encampment, and garbage heap that the most anyone could do was to try to keep his senses, watch out for the guards, steer clear of the man with delirium tremens, jump out of the way of the man who vomited his stew, or in other ways protect himself; worrying about one's neighbor's origin in Europe or Africa or Asia was not practical.

When we were examined for venereal disease, everybody appeared in the same line. No separate line for the Negroes. When we were assigned beds it went the same way, with white and Negro sleeping in adjoining cots. All night long in that great large bedroom, where perhaps a thousand men snored, roared, fought, dreamed aloud, I sat up in bed staring about with incredulity to see what the city of New York and America had wrought. The lights were dimmed, but still one could see the vermin crawling. On all sides men scratched and scratched and picked off the multi-typed lice. But I heard no one insult anyone else for color or background. All was reduced to an animal level and all was equal.

True, this was the equality and the integration of decadence and death.

Yet in the life of this reporter and student of Negro-white relations, nowhere else have I ever seen such full integration when it was not an "experiment" or a matter of sufferance to someone, as it is in the church, the school system, the political, economic, and cultural life of the nation.

The curious thing about the whole issue of integration is that not only the Negro is striving for it. In a way the whole nation is reaching for an integrated understanding, each ethnic element with the other. It is only that in the attainment of this objective the Negro meets up with the principal resistance.

Possibly the main conflict in America still remains that of capital versus the so-called "common man," but a strong secondary cross-current of antagonism definitely exists between the Anglo-Saxon mainstream of America and the more than one-third of the nation which is non-Anglo-Saxon—the one-third made up of the Irish, Jewish, Spanish, Polish, French, Russian, Portuguese, German, Mexican, American Indian, Balkan, and Baltic groups, Orientals, Latin Americans, and others. In addition to this bloc there is that one-tenth of the nation which is Negro, often in conflict with the heterogeneous one-third as well as with the traditional Anglo-Saxon group. Religious outlooks, particularly of Roman Catholic and Jewish groups, also figure importantly in the picture.

The physical existence of a national minority segment of the population does not mean that there is necessarily a political alignment against the traditional white-Anglo-Saxon-Protestant bloc. Neither is there anything like a group homogeneity in the Anglo-Saxon ranks of the nation. The Civil War showed how this population could be split, and how, on sectional matters, it differs to this day. The minorities too are split; there are Irish and Jewish capitalists and Irish and Jewish labor leaders. Two Negro leaders in the state of Georgia backed Eugene Talmadge for governor in 1946. Italian workers who came to the U.S.A. around the turn of the century at the urging of great industrialists very often cling to the conservative grouping. Jews can be found in all parties: they range from radical to reactionary. That a few Irish priests

163]

and some of their following are sympathetic to fascism is well known. Then the issue of civil liberties for religious groups and the chronic campaign of the Klan against Catholics has tended to move many Catholics over into an area of suspicion and opposition to the Klan wing of Anglo-Protestantism.

The main influence working on this "unintegrated bloc" is the force of organized labor. It was in this area that President Roosevelt found so much of the strength and backing for his New Deal program. A look at the roll of labor leadership today very frequently shows names that stem from recent immigrant groups. This is understandable when one realizes that such men came here as an infusion into the labor strength of the nation, and that consequently labor and progressive ideas in the main attracted them.

This whole matter has been best expressed by Louis Adamic, who, for fifteen years, has been trying to make America conscious of its *potential* "melting pot" nature. He has put forward his thesis that the cultural pattern of America is not essentially Anglo-Saxon, even though the Anglo-Saxon occupies a great, backbone-like position in the body of the nation. The pattern of America, he says, is a blend of the cultures of the world. Diversity is the American pattern, and one of the most important sources of the nation's strength. Mr. Adamic brought this thought to fruition in his *A Nation of Nations* which, not pretending to be an economic-political history of the country, still conveyed the concept of diversity as the pattern of America, thus breaking the ground for a realization of the existence of neglected areas of democratic upsurge.

My experience with Negro America tends strongly to confirm such a position. No one could walk the streets of Harlem daily, seeing in the faces that pass the mingling of the peoples of the whole world, and not perceive great truth in the Adamic viewpoint. In fact, I believe that it is in the Negro American where the melting-pot theory is exemplified most completely. What this

[164

means is that one cannot truly speak any longer of a "Negro" or a "black" man or a "colored" person. The people of color, with the world poured into their veins, may well be carrying the heritage of some new America now rushing upon us.

The tide of mixing, integrating, amalgamating—whatever it may be called—has been pouring over America in the last few years like waters that have broken a dam. The theatre and literature have very clearly reflected this ethnic consciousness. *Common Ground,* a magazine of the melting-pot character, has for years printed articles showing the rise and struggle of national and color groups. The annual "I Am An American Day" always educes "the pattern of diversity." Earl Robinson arose in music as an expression of the fact that an American can be an international human type.

The Negro theme is at the core of this movement, like the seeds in an apple.

Theoretically all national minorities should be working in close harmony with the Negro toward common political ends. But when riots directed against the Negro group have broken out, all too often, in the North at least, the white assailants have issued from other minority groupings. Competition in the sphere of labor and the struggle to secure decent housing have usually been at the root of such clashes. Restricted housing, directed also against the immigrant groups, has served to breed in some of these nationals the prejudices of the dominant class, so that they too vent the wrath of insecurity upon an already bedeviled people. Reactionary forces like the Klan have taken advantage of these tensions to incite clashes with the Negro. The Jewish, in general, understand the Negro's plight intellectually, and many individuals and some organizations of recent have been agitating for some kind of political cohesiveness with the Negro. In the main, Jewish religious leadership has failed to press this sufficiently. The Jewish trade unionist has been way ahead of the synagogue in stretching forth a hand.

It would be difficult to make political forecasts about this amorphous gathering of ethnic and national minorities, but there is a general feeling that both theoretically and practically it has something in common—a need for standing together.

If the free-enterprise nations speak of a world without wars, or of an ultimate aim of peace in a warring world, as they often do; if the labor movement of the world speaks of a society without classes, as it often does; then the Negro people also speak of an objective which they have: an American society without segregation. Such a society would be an integrated one. This is just as revolutionary an objective for the American scene as the objective of a classless society is for the world scene. When one considers how far outside the main American pattern the Negro people finds itself, then one can understand how the drive toward this objective is fraught with all the drama of the world struggle of labor, capital, nations, and colonies. Our internal Negro-white fight is a dramatic flank of the whole international conflict. Although the Negro drives toward integration in the business, professional, religious, and social life of the nation, perhaps primarily he moves into the labor area of America. Here, too, there is struggle, for the black man and woman do not have an easy time entering fully into the trade-union movement. In the South, for example, white workers are not at all free of supremacist ideas. On the West Coast, during the war, Negro and white workers were often organized into separate unions. In particular the Negro has a fight on his hands in the American Federation of Labor. But the Negro is, in the main, a workingman. He meets white workers, belongs to unions composed chiefly of whites. So his drive toward "full integration" perhaps takes its most significant shape in the labor area. Complete participation in the trade-union movement is the first condition for his entry into the full life of white America.

It is right to say, finally, that the measure of the advance of white Americans toward full democracy is determined by the progress which the Negro makes in achieving integration. To the extent that the person of color secures the same rights and opportunities as white people in a church, public meeting, labor union, theatre, residential area, or any other institution, to that extent white Americans themselves become democratized. To the extent that the Negro meets up with denial, it is white America which lags behind in the achievement of the "Century of the Common Man."

In so very many areas of American society, since the beginning of World War II, there has occurred so much integration that it can no longer be said there are two solid groups, or worlds, left in the land. In spite of the great evil of segregation districts in most cities of the nation, and a whole edifice of Jim Crow still fairly intact, a significant interpenetration of Negro and white institutions has also occurred. The phenomena indicative of this would fill a book. As Dr. Herbert Aptheker, an authority on Negro-white relations, put it to me recently, "I think the gains of the Negro people during the war and as a result of the victory achieved have already been enormous." The whole scene has been filled with "firsts." A Negro man enters the Hall of Fame, a Negro woman is selected as the "Mother of the Year," a colored man is elected to a new office on the federal bench, the Supreme Court reverses itself on the question of Negro rights in a Jim Crow bus in interstate traffic, and so on. One thousand Negroes and whites meet in a Southern Negro church, indiscriminately seated. Such things did not occur a few years ago.

The principle of integration has, by now, been shot like a flight of arrows into most American institutions. It has even penetrated the hidebound South so that it can no longer be said there is a Solid South. Not even politically is there a Democratic, white-primary Solid South. In state after state the process of erosion working on traditional principles has taken its toll in sundered political groupings, realignments, attitudes. I asked a Southern authority to give me a percentage estimate of the influence of white supremacy today in the general territory called the South. He attempted it this way: "About thirty per cent might be pretty militant in favor of racist thinking. Another forty per cent are relatively neutral or in-different or uncertain. The other thirty per cent don't like it. This doesn't mean that the latter thirty per cent are all actively fighting against the caste-restrictive setup any more than the thirty per cent at the other extreme are actively warring to spread white su-premacy. I don't know what the percentage would be at either extreme of political actives. But the South has some such three-way political character as that right now."

To give emphasis to the changes going on in the South it can be said that there is an enveloping movement of progressive think-ing in the North, which spreads into and around the South. The serious campaign of organized labor, long a Northern movement primarily, in the South is the main manifestation of this anti-racist process. The church in the North trying to make itself Christian has finally made some inroads on the Southern Christian mind. For centuries there was a real, albeit incredible, belief that Chris-tianity and color prejudice were quite compatible. While this is still the belief of the Eugene Talmadge Christians, it has been badly shattered in other sections of the Southern church.

Mostly it is in the army of interracial organizations in the North where the revolution (it may be such) is taking place. There is the Springfield Plan, evolved in Springfield, Massachusetts, where the entire community, under educational leadership, participates in in-tergroup efforts. There is A. Ritchie Low's project in Vermont. Within labor organizations education for group understanding has risen to its highest level. In one recent case in the National Maritime Union, seventeen white members were expelled from the union for refusing to ship out with Negro seamen. The Com-munist Party rigidly looks for what it calls "chauvinism," their technical-political term for white supremacy, in its white members. There is no question but that this party, perhaps more than any other, has given the most serious attention to cleansing its white membership of the attitudes of prejudice.

In the major political parties freedom from prejudice is more likely an individual manifestation than a matter of party policy.

Arthur B. Spingarn, president of the National Association for the Advancement of Colored People, told me a story about the late Wendell Willkie illustrative of this. It seems that when Spingarn first met Willkie, the latter was very weak on the Negro question. Willkie, riding in a cab with Spingarn sometime before the 1940 elections, revealed that he had only a very practical approach to the question, one based simply on votes. Perhaps it was his defeat in 1940, when the Negro vote went heavily to Roosevelt, that taught Willkie something. Whatever it was, said Spingarn, Willkie grew in the 1940's. Before he died he felt the Negro issue strongly and had good understanding of it and a feeling of warmth for Negroes.

Henry Wallace's forthright stand on the issue of the poll tax and FEPC in the Democratic Party was sufficient to rule him out of Vice-presidential consideration by the influential Southern Bourbon wing.

My point is: sympathy in the major parties has been an individual matter, or a matter of political opportunism. It is significant that members of both major parties combined to destroy Fair Employment Practices Committee legislation. That is why Negroes have for years eyed left-wing movements as the most fruitful areas for the development of understanding of group by group.

In many places organizations like the National Urban League and the National Association for the Advancement of Colored People have meetings and activities in which whites, in numbers, participate. A common practice in American small towns, that of having interracial councils of white and Negro leadership to take up community problems, has had its effect. Sometimes the Negro element on such councils has been conciliatory and has militated against the Negro group, but in the present period these councils usually secure gains.

New York City has *hundreds* of such organizations. Almost

every neighborhood has its interracial communities, or intercultural committees. Parents, teachers, religionists, labor officials are the most active. "Tension areas" in most big cities now have intergroup committees working to educate whites in such neighborhoods, smooth out difficulties as they arise, and prevent such tensions from becoming serious. White America has begun work on a white American problem.

I wish I could say that taking the road toward happy social understanding with the Negro has been a casual matter for me. Then I could write some idyllic story in which I might claim immunity from the conditioning factors of the environment, or recite some purely subjective yarn wherein I would say: "Well, I simply hit it off smoothly with Negroes. I always did and I always will." I wish it had been as simple at that, but it has not been. It has been a fight. If it were as easy as that for a white man to associate with Negroes, then he would be living in a different world, or a different country, or some place where our present standards do not prevail, and such a story as this would not have to be told. Contrariwise, for me to have integrated myself with the Negro community means that I have had to pass through a snarling undergrowth of white prejudice, hatred, misconceptions, frequent Negro mistrust, and personal stumbling blocks. I have had to pass through this, hack it out of my way, drive poisonous ideas out of my own system, and tangle with the mammoth of Jim Crow—a modern beast fully as dangerous in our time and country as the dinosaur was in its period.

I suspect that the whole of America is also going through some such struggle, through some internal economic-political bath, some conflict of the soul, the mind, and the body.

Until this process is completed, with whom else can men and women of good will stand, other than Langston Hughes who says:

> Out of the rack and ruin of our gangster death,
> The rape and rot of graft, and stealth, and lies,

THE PRINCIPLE OF INTEGRATION

We, the people, must redeem
The land, the mines, the plants, the rivers,
The mountains and the endless plain—
All, all the stretch of these great green states—
And make America again!

CHAPTER FOURTEEN

THE NEGRO, STATES' RIGHTS, AND
THE MAJOR PARTIES

"Mr. Dewey led the fight that broke Wendell Willkie's heart."
—FORMER GOVERNOR HERBERT H. LEHMAN
in the *N.Y. Post,* Oct. 21st, 1946.

THIS is the story of the Negro's relationship to the political realignments going on currently in the major parties.

I begin with two apocryphal stories illustrative of sectional attitudes, or as I choose to call the issue here: the question of states' rights.

Senator Theodore Bilbo was taking a drink at the bar of the Waldorf-Astoria in New York. "Suh," said Bilbo to the bartender, "Ah wish to order a jigger of bourbon." A *PM* reporter standing next to the senator turned and abruptly addressed him thus: "Sir, I'll have you know that up here we say 'Jigro.'"

Still another one circulates around about the Southern Congressman who, interviewed on his sixtieth birthday, was asked by a reporter, "You've been in Congress for a long time, haven't you, sir?" The representative replied: "Ah shuah have. Just about twenty-fahv yeahs." The reporter continued, "Then you've seen some mighty big changes, haven't you?" And the answer came, "Yeah, and Ah've been against them all."

The traditional differences in North-South attitudes continue. There may be as much of a sectional problem today as a century ago, when Yankee and Southerner faced each other across the border states. For a time it was fashionable to think that the wounds of the Civil War were healed nationally, and there was no longer any major issue between the North and the South. Yet if that were true the South would not be so vociferous today in its guardianship of the same states' rights theory which, in a measure, brought the nation to arms in 1861. If that were true then I would not have heard from the lips of so many Northern white veterans who trained in the South their dislike of Southern attitudes and economic backwardness.

In 1799, only a few years after the ratification of the Constitution, the states' rights issue first appeared. This was the position that states had the right to nullify acts of Congress if they believed or wanted to believe that they were unconstitutional. Kentucky and Virginia, opposing the Alien and Sedition Acts, contended that if the federal government overshot its constitutional limits, one state or a group of states could repudiate the federal power. From that time until this day the states' rights contention has flared across our history like some star-spangled comet. The states' rights principle became a catch basin for the slave power soon after its initial utterance. As the Northern states increased in industrial strength, as the free-labor system began to outpace the slave system, the Southern states more and more relied upon their local power to oppose anti-slavery and free-labor legislation. By the year 1820 the states' rights principle became a legal arm and argument for the maintenance of slavery. In that year, through an agreement between Northern and Southern members of Congress, the territory of Missouri was admitted to the Union as a slave state. From that day to this Congressmen both North and South have been bartering Negro lives for one political expediency or another. To use a hackneyed image, states' rights compromises became one side of the coin of which Negro oppression was the other. In 1833 the state of South Carolina invoked the states' rights principle and threatened secession if the federal government did not offer a lower tariff to the South. South Carolina actually prepared to secede and become a nation on and of its own. The tariff issue was an organic facet of the slave empire and of that system's conflict with the free-labor setup of the North. In the 1850's states' rights was invoked by Southern legislators to maintain the slave institution in their own states, to spread it to the West, and to deny the Negro all citizenship rights. Finally, this principle was tested on the battlefield; the North won, and ostensibly the meaning was that no state could secede, or establish laws which went contrary to the Constitution.

But the biggest compromise of all was destined to occur a few years after the close of the Civil War. Once more states' rights was to be restored to national life as a principle which the South could employ to "keep the Negro in his place." This was the famous "gentlemen's agreement" of 1876, by which Rutherford B. Hayes, Ohio Republican, was named to the presidency after he secured a tie vote in the electoral college with the South's Democratic candidate, Samuel J. Tilden. The story of this compromise is now widely known, for it formed the crux of one of Howard Fast's most important novels, *Freedom Road*. The agreement was to allow Hayes to assume the presidency in exchange for granting the Southern Democrats the right to restore white supremacist control of the South. Hayes's first act after he became President was to withdraw federal troops from the South. As soon as the military protection for the Reconstruction legislatures was withdrawn, the Klan and the Democratic Party by violence occupied one state capitol building after another and the restoration of the "slavocracy" was completed. The Negro and his white allies were thrown backward, and white supremacist states' rights was again in the saddle.

Now, that political deal is one of the most important for an understanding of the Negro aspect of the democratic question today. Practically everything in the modern Jim Crow system traces to that hour when the major parties agreed, as they had many times before, to abandon the Negro for the sake of sectional, party, or class harmony. The 1876 compromise became a pattern for a Democratic-Republican alliance that has continued in American politics until now. The most salient fact in American politics today is the Republican-Democrat Congressional coalition. This Congressional alliance became so significant in 1946 that on many sides the two major parties were viewed as in reality one, and the possibility of a third party presented itself. The major manifestations of Democrat-Republican agreement have been in the form of Southern legislators taking the offensive against labor in the North while the Northern Republicans sabotaged reform proposals intended to advance the South, such as poll-tax abolition and fair-employment practices. Thus the "gentlemen's agreement" of the Reconstruction period had become more or less continuous over the generations.

How does all this link up with the Negro and his relationship to the major parties?

When in 1876 the Republicans, who had championed the Negro ever since 1856, started the trek backward, their betrayal marked a turning point in American history. For the Negro it meant that the rate of his progress was slashed by about ninety per cent. Had the Republicans at that time persisted in guarding Negro rights in the South it is possible that the Negro in 1947 would have had at least the status of the white workingman, and in some cases of the middle class. Right now the Negro does not possess that. Negro workers and those of middle-class income, and even the scattering of wealthy Negroes, all live under restricted conditions as a people apart. Actually the stories that circulate, to the effect that the Negro has made a greater advance in seventy-five years than any other people ever just emerged from slavery, are false. Such talk is the

175]

defense argument of benevolent civic administration unwilling to hasten up processes which would enlarge the Negro's scope of freedom. The Negro's few advances, primarily in education, were made almost independently, and practically without the assistance of either major party; on the contrary, in the face of betrayal and conscious opposition by the decisive elements in both parties. If the Negro has been able to point to a few educational and property gains in seventy-five years of a dubious "emancipation" he can also say, "If the Republicans had not sold us out we might today be totally free of Jim Crow controls."

After 1876 the South established its "Two World" relationship. It passed hundreds of discrimination laws effective in every sphere of white and Negro life, it disfranchised the Negro (and six million poor whites, too), it intermittently employed violence to maintain its segregation system, and in general rigidly stood in the path of Negro advance. Instead of free enterprise taking root in the South there developed the economic fungus growths of sharecropping and peonage, and there appeared a mule-agrarian economy which was torn between its late parent, slavery, and the pull of Northern industry. In the North the Republicans turned to the pursuit of industry and forgot the social cause on which they had ridden to power. The abolitionists began to lose strength and die away. Booker T. Washington appeared and told the Negro to steer clear of politics and not seek social equality with whites: just work hard, buy property, and build your own society. A split in the woman suffrage movement sometime earlier, in 1868, had torn from the Negro his traditional ally of unfranchised white women. By 1900 the Negro was forgotten by most white political interests in the country (except where it was necessary to oppose Negro advance), and the process of shunting him off to his side of the community was pretty well completed everywhere. The Negro lived very much unto himself until the Roosevelt administration came along and, once again, the nation began to hear of "peons," "Jim Crow," "sharecroppers," "Scottsboro boys," and "the caste-outs."

NEGRO, STATES' RIGHTS, AND MAJOR PARTIES

The repeated election of Roosevelt to the presidency became unendurable to the Republican Party. It finally projected Wendell Willkie, who attempted to out-Roosevelt Roosevelt and out-New Deal the New Deal. And the closer Willkie came to his "One World" position and to the discovery of liberalism, the closer he had to come to the Negro. He came nearest in 1940 when the Negroes broke cleanly with their Republican past, voted overwhelmingly for Roosevelt, and helped defeat Willkie.

After 1940 Wendell Willkie began to issue pro-Negro pronouncements. The Negroes, anxious for any and all allies, and glad to hear someone speak out again in the party that had emancipated them as well as forgotten them, encouraged Willkie.

What did this mean? It meant that Wendell Willkie was the first Republican since 1876 to raise the Negro question again inside that party. Willkie had broken the "gentlemen's agreement" between the two major parties to keep quiet on the Negro. Willkie had become "treasonable" to the traditional North-South alliance. Willkie had dumped the Negro question back into the lap of his party and he had brought to fruition a process that Roosevelt had begun back in 1936, when the latter declared the South to be Economic Problem Number One. Willkie was in a spot where he had to outdo, in words, the pro-Negro deeds of the Roosevelt administration. This wasn't too difficult a task. The Negro made gains in the Roosevelt period, not because Roosevelt personally or directly did so very much for the Negro, because "he never said a mumblin' word," but the job he was doing for the "common man" everywhere drew the Negro into its progressive orbit. Roosevelt had allowed labor to organize and grow and when that process began the Negro could make progress too.

Willkie came along, trailing this process, and trying to outdo it. Let us see what happened.

When a young man named Thomas E. Dewey took office as Governor of New York State shortly before the start of the present decade, he stated, in a way that historians and party leaders and the South could understand, that he wanted to be President of the United States. He told *official* America that he would not tamper with the Negro question. He would let the South go its traditional way. He would carry on as an 1876 Republican guaranteeing the Republican *and* Democratic South what President Rutherford B. Hayes had guaranteed before: that the South could handle the Negro people in its own way if and when he became President.

Now did Dewey say it in just those words? No. He did not have to. All that he had to do was to say over and over again that he was a guarantor of states' rights. That he did. His historian advisers told him to take a firm stand on the states' rights question and *everybody who needed to know* would understand just where he stood and just what he meant. Dewey peppered his earliest gubernatorial speeches with clauses about preserving states' rights. The South listened with interest. The Republican Party took note. After 1940, the party leadership knew that Dewey was throwing down the gauntlet to Wendell Willkie. Willkie had broken the "gentlemen's agreement" of 1876, and Dewey had reaffirmed it! Dewey had announced himself as a right-wing Republican candidate for the presidency while Willkie was holding up the left wing. *The Negro had become the issue determining left and right, but it was suggested only subtly by Dewey in the form of his repeated assurances about states' rights.*

There were those, unaware of the historical implications, unaware of the growing clash of right and left in Republican ranks, who wondered, "Why is Thomas Dewey talking about states' rights?" "Where," they asked, "inside New York State, is there any issue of states' rights or any need to discuss the principle?" "For whom is he speaking?" Or, "Against whom is he speaking?" Those who wondered what Dewey was talking about without seeing clearly where he was headed reasoned that the Empire State was the wealthiest, its population was the largest, and it had more strength in Washington, in federal government, and in the making

[178

of national policy than any other state. Since states' rights has always been the recourse of smaller states, and practically always Southern states, why was Dewey raising the issue before the people of New York?

Actually, Dewey was talking for consumption down South, especially to Southern Republicans, and making his bid for the 1944 Republican presidential nomination.

Only one man in American history before Dewey had proclaimed states' rights with anything like the vehemence of the young Republican. This was John C. Calhoun, that ardent slavery advocate who one hundred years before arose in Congress to declare "Slavery is right," and to forecast secession and war. How did it happen that, a century later, a young Northern Republican began to echo states' rights talk?

It was as historian that I became aware of the strange, three-generation-old drama unfolding within the Republican Party, and it was as journalist that I had the opportunity to have some very slight connection with the process itself.

I was on *PM* when Dewey was making ready to stand back of his states' rights position with a deed. He had extradited one escaped Negro prisoner to Georgia over the protest of New York Negroes, but that action was not considered sufficient to assure the South that he would not touch their caste system should be become president. The Southern Republicans demanded something more from Dewey before he would get their votes at the 1944 nominating convention. The issue presented itself in the spring session of the New York Legislature of 1944.

A certain measure, the Anti-Discrimination Bill, was introduced to the Legislature. Prepared by the Anti-Discrimination Commission, a group of prominent liberals, it was the state's version of the Fair Employment Practices Committee measures which came about during the war as a result of a series of Roosevelt decrees. The state had especial need for such a law. New York City was the seat of many large minorities, Negro, Jewish, Irish, Italian, and others. Discrimination in employment had always existed there against one group or another. The proposed measure would outlaw such discrimination and provide a fine for employers found guilty of biased practices. It was understood that, in the main, this would help the Negro, but at the same time, it would provide a guarantee for others of various national and religious groupings. There was a certain amount of pressure to get Dewey to enact the measure into law at the spring 1944 session of the Legislature. But no great public movement. Perhaps it was not an especially vigorous campaign because it never occurred to anyone that Dewey would risk not passing this legislation, *the principal measure before the Legislature*, just before he expected to secure the Republican nomination. But Dewey faced a dilemma. If he made this pro-Negro, pro-minority measure into law, he would antagonize the conservative Southern element and repudiate his earlier states' rights talk. If he passed the measure he might get the Negro vote in the metropolitan area, but he might *not* get the nomination of the Southern Republicans, which he needed. He decided he must convince the supremacist-minded Southern Republican electors that he would not, if he became president, interfere with their continuing use of the Negro as a source of cheap labor and high rentals.

So when the Governor reported to the Legislature on the Anti-Discrimination Bill, instead of urging its immediate passage, he said that the issue of prejudice against minorities in employment needed more study. He recommended that the study be made and the bill be dropped for a year—until the spring 1945 session of the Legislature. That would be after the election, and by that time, Dewey hoped, he would be president, and it wouldn't matter to him what New York State did about the measure.

Within a few hours of the time when Dewey was before the New York State Legislature, dropping Negro and minority rights, his right-hand man, Lieutenant Governor Joseph R. Hanley, made a "keynote Republican speech," as the New York *Times* index lists it for March 17, 1944, in Charlotte, North Carolina, before the Legislature of that state. Hanley told the Southerners that Dewey's election in 1944 would make the country secure in the postwar world. It was tacitly understood that the South was to take note of how Dewey was concurrently handling the Anti-Discrimination measure. The whole deal was just as neat, just as gentlemanly, an agreement as the original Hayes-Tilden, Democrat-Republican deal of 1876. History had presented the American people once more with a classic example of compromise at the expense primarily of the blood and bread of the Negro one-tenth.

The move was fully exposed at the time. It boomeranged and turned on the young Republican and hit him harder than he had ever been hit with anything before. Most of all, *PM* disclosed the meaning of the maneuver—*even down to the original compromise deal way back in 1876.* I recall writing a number of stories for that paper about the whole business, and I remember telephoning friends on the Negro press in various parts of the country and conveying to them the meaning of Dewey's position. The *Defender*, with which I was not then associated, wired me asking the significance of the situation and I replied with a statement conveying its historic background much as I have described it here.

Dewey lost the election. He also discovered that in eight Northern states the Negro voting bloc is populous enough to be decisive in a presidential campaign. Later, in 1945, Dewey allowed the Anti-Discrimination Bill to become law and tried to recoup ground by making a number of Negro appointments. But I am not concerned with the merits of Dewey then and now. My point is, that with Dewey's maneuvering, the Negro question, clothed in the legal term *states' rights*, came back to America in full strength for the first time since 1876. While Dewey played to the right and assured the nation he would never seriously move against Jim Crow in the South, it was the great contribution of Wendell Willkie that he broke with this tradition, forced Dewey to take a stand on the Negro, and brought back to the Republicans a reawareness of the tradition on which it rose to power.

After Willkie's death not one voice arose in the Republican Party to take up where he left off. I was with the *Defender* by then, and, looking for some Republican with even a slightly liberal record to take some kind of a progressive position on Negro rights, I sought out Clare Boothe Luce. Unwilling to grant a personal interview, she described her position at length in a letter, and we printed her statement in a full-page layout. She made a valiant attempt to express herself liberally, but her answers were politically weak, and in my column I described her as a poor substitute in Republican ranks for Willkie. I asked her to call on her party to break the coalition with the Southern Democrats. Neither she nor her party severed that relationship, and the editor of my paper, Dr. Metz Lochard, turned in disgust from the party of Mrs. Luce and the illiberal regime of President Truman and called for a third party. This was the first of a long series of third-party repercussions that followed throughout the country.

The states' rights issue covertly manifested itself inside the Democratic Party nominating convention in 1944 too. When Henry Wallace came out for abolition of the poll tax and a federal Fair Employment Practices Act he came to grips with the states' rights bloc in his own party. A senator named Harry Truman of Missouri won out. But Wallace's progressive stand had projected the Negro question to the forefront inside the Democratic Party too, and, as with the Republicans, it was a crucial issue at the nominating convention. It was an interesting confirmation of the historic process of Republican-Democrat agreement that the compromise stand which Dewey took on the Negro helped him win the Republican nomination while Wallace's pro-Negro position largely lost the nomination for him among Democrats.

There stands the issue of states' rights, the legal protector of Jim Crow at the moment. It cuts across both major parties. It projects Negro rights to the propeller position of American life. Always the

NEGRO, STATES' RIGHTS, AND MAJOR PARTIES

Negro has been pivotal in American politics. It has never been possible to compromise the question and ignore it for very long. Negro pressure for justice combined with the rivalries of political groups have ever conspired to bring it into the open at crucial periods. And each time the issue has been aired white sections and classes have split and the Negro has poured through to new advances.

There may be no Solid South, but there is still a boiling sectional conflict. That antagonism is bridged now by labor-capital relations North and South. What will this complex of factors adduce for the near future? Will the Rankin element attempt another secession movement and attempt to set up its own nation in some new Confederacy, to suppress Negro and white progressive advance? It is always possible. Is it possible that the Negro and white allies North and South could take over the states' rights theory and use it themselves for continuous democratic advance? That too is possible. All that I know is that the major parties have been rocking, but in an inward way, with the repercussions of this traditional conflict between the individual Southern states and the federal government. I think it time to bring the matter out into the open.

CHAPTER FIFTEEN

WHO LEADS THE NEGRO?

"The American Council on Race Relations reaffirms the American principle of free and independent labor unions. The history of the American labor movement has proved it to be one of the most effective forces in advancing democratic race relations. As the labor movement has grown in stature and independence the lot of minorities has correspondingly improved. What affects labor directly affects the welfare of minorities. The labor movement must be kept free and independent and any efforts to put arbitrary limits on labor's freedom of action represents a direct threat to minority interests."

—STATEMENT ON THE OCCASION OF THE 1946 CIO AND AFL ORGANIZING DRIVE IN THE SOUTH.

IT IS in the nature of the Negro relationship to the American scene that the people of color are compelled to rely to a great extent on political progressivism among white Americans. Since the nation is overwhelmingly peopled with whites, this is the bloc which, if it is at war, takes the Negro to war also; and if it is involved in a depression, the Negro is, even before others, in that depression, too. By the same token, if there is a dead silence

[184

throughout the white world on Negro issues, then the Negro bloc, with all its protest, is in somewhat the position of a tide rolling up to a powerful wall, and just sliding backward. For years, from about 1900 to 1930, the Negro, despite great activity in his own behalf, despite great protest, and an occasional bloody demonstration, was unable to shake America into any serious realization of its supremacist behavior. It was not until forces rose within the white world—notably labor organization, World War II, and minority group agitation for ethnic democracy—that the protest of the Negro began to register with any great effect.

This was more or less a duplication of a similar occurrence in the early life of the nation when the Negro was a slave and when, in the main, white America ignored the Negro. Benjamin Franklin expressed himself against slavery, and to some extent his stand was a factor, but there was no very great movement or political organization to accompany his espousal of fraternity. The Quakers opposed slavery in the pre-Constitutional period and afterward too, but they were an isolated sect, and the very fact that they did advocate anti-slavery was sufficient to drive other groups away from alliance with them. And when, in the Constitution itself, we allowed the slave trade to remain with us until 1808, this was open acceptance and maintenance of the slave institution, and it meant that *official* white America had no intention of *leading* in its removal. It remained for individual whites to set anti-slavery processes into motion while at the same time Negroes engaged in an unending series of abortive slave revolts and escapes to the North in their attempt to secure freedom and focus attention on the evil. In the colonial and post-Revolutionary life of our country, the pressures of rising industrialism apparently were not here in sufficient force to make slavery incompatible with the organization of capitalism at that stage and in that period. It was not until the third or fourth decade of the nineteenth century that it became evident the needs of an expanding free enterprise economy were coming to grips with the system of slavery.

About 1810 a white man named Benjamin Lundy started organizing anti-slavery societies and issuing a periodical called *The Genius of Universal Emancipation*. It was a significant title for a periodical, for it was in the Tom Paine tradition and it was a rediscovery of universal equities at a moment in the national development when we were chiefly bent upon domestic and isolationist thinking. Just as thinking in international terms in our day drove Wendell Willkie to a specific consideration of the Negro here so, in that earlier time, Lundy's international outlook compelled him to view the slave question as the integral American problem. Lundy's activity led to the William Lloyd Garrison movement. And Garrison's abolitionism stood, as the years passed, alongside a several-fronted movement for emancipation of the Negro.

Then, Negro revolts, the Underground Railroad, parliamentary reform, the theory of disunion, the militant John Brown wing of the abolitionist cause, and finally the very important free-soil movement, merged to become one large rolling force which would ultimately liberate the Negro from his property status. White leaders like Garrison, Wendell Phillips, Harriet Beecher Stowe, Theodore Parker, Salmon Chase, Joshua Giddings, and scores of others exerted a determining influence on white Americans. White churchmen and white laborers threw their support to the broad, gathering anti-slavery tide. It was a "New Deal" period. Joined with these individual and group forces was a list of notable Negro leaders: Frederick Douglass, Martin Delany, James McCune Smith, Sojourner Truth, Frances Watkins Harper, and many others who gave inspiration to both Negro and white.

But leadership was primarily a matter of movements, rather than individuals, even if individuals symbolized and directed certain processes. Finally, in that period, it was Abraham Lincoln who can be said, in the greatest measure, to have led the Negro, even though he was, as Frederick Douglass put it, "the white man's President." Lincoln was the instrument of an historic process of advance, a process which placed the Negro in Lincoln's path.

WHO LEADS THE NEGRO?

The pattern of joint white-Negro leadership of the Negro continues in our own time. Negro leaders recognize that the power to make change rests, in considerable measure, upon the readiness for action and re-understanding of large sections of white America. Thus the Negro finds himself often in the position of prodding white labor and liberal leadership to get into motion on Negro rights. The Negro, meantime, is inclined to take help from wherever he can receive it, and that is why he accepted the contribution of Willkie among Republicans, Wallace and Ickes among Democrats, and that is why he also works with white Labor, Independent, Communist, and Socialist leadership.

I was discussing the question of leadership with an informed Negro acquaintance recently, and he made the statement that practically all of the current leaders, certainly those who wield the most influence in the Negro community, had their origins in and have a more or less continuing relationship to labor-left schools of thinking. I think this is true. The Negro's position has been one of too great submergence for Negro leaders to entertain much hope their people will find liberation within the world of things as they are. The most significant national Negro leaders for the last generation have had to provide answers and militancy which cannot stem from but must lead away from the feudal-property rights way of life of either Senator Bilbo in the South or the chronic industrial unemployment situation in the North. There should be nothing surprising in this. There is no more reason to expect hope and confidence and faith in our present economy from a mass as excluded from its benefits as the Negro American than faith in the British Empire from the Malayan.

I was discussing the growing labor-left internationalism of the Negro American recently with the poet, Melvin Tolson, who teaches at Wiley College in Texas. A man informed in political economy, he took the position that if and when a leader or a movement arose in America that the Negro followed, it would be a white man and primarily a white progressive movement. He put

187]

it even more specifically than that, saying, "The man who leads the Negroes right now is Philip Murray." I would not agree unreservedly to that, for it is too categorical and the Congress of Industrial Organizations is itself a split force. I think that what is important in Tolson's observation, and what is really the sense of his statement, is that white labor, wherever it is truly progressive, leads the Negro. There may be little consolation in that for business, if business hopes that it has the confidence of the Negro, but there has been little consolation for the Negro in three hundred years of subjection to a political and legal structure evolved by slaveholding, industrial, and property interests, which "included the Negro out."

It may have been evident as far back as 1936 that the Negro was following white labor and struggling for an equal position within that movement, but any doubt about the decisive role of labor in the life of the Negro vanished after the CIO and AFL organizing campaigns began in the South in 1946. Not that these drives held out hope of bringing any very immediate "racial" advance to the Negro. But it meant that an historical process in operation all over the world for the last century, the struggle of labor to organize, had finally penetrated in a large way one of the last strongholds of world feudalism, Dixie. The Negro Southerner had been praying for this for years, and at last it came, weakly and uncertainly, but it came.

This direct connection between the Negro and white labor, and the reliance of the Negro, as of all minorities, upon this relationship, was illustrated when the American Council on Race Relations took note of this organizing drive and reaffirmed its support of "the American principle of free and independent labor unions" and the progressive effect of labor on "democratic race relations." On the board of this organization are such diverse class and group interests as those represented by Louis Adamic, Marshall Field, Bishop William Scarlett, Walter White, Abraham Rubin, Clarence

E. Pickett, and others typical of the nation's social, religious, and ethnic segments.

Although progressive white labor is the focal spot on which the eyes of the Negro are now centered, the Negro desires participation in the *full* fabric of the American scheme, and he looks with hungry eyes on the interracial advancement efforts of any and all whites in the political, industrial, cultural, and religious worlds. When, for example, the annual Negro College Fund campaign takes place, sponsored by John D. Rockefeller, Jr. and Thomas A. Morgan of the Sperry Corporation and other such big business figures, this effort gets the fairly complete support of the Negro. If the Federal Council of Churches of Christ announces that segregation will be combatted in their churches until it is ended (as it did recently), then the Negro recognizes this as a step forward too, and he is grateful for such white church leadership. The search for admission to the white world, and for friends and leaders in white areas, goes on on a front three thousand miles wide, from border to border.

But, as Harold Preece, an astute observer of Southern conditions, once remarked, "The trade-union movement has done more for democratic group relations in the South than three hundred years of the church."

A number of years ago I had a most interesting correspondence with Carrie Chapman Catt, who led the battle for woman suffrage in its final stages. A woman of philosophic breadth and great social grasp, and in the nature of her reformist profession a liberal, she would, I felt, possess an enlightened attitude toward the Negro. But I found she had limited understanding and that she possessed a distinctly limited knowledge of Negro-white relations. When Mrs. Catt made the statement that "The Negroes had no leadership then [in the anti-slavery period] and they have very little now," I saw how far she was from having real information, and I was moved to make reply in a six-page, single-spaced, type-written letter.

I pointed out to Mrs. Catt that the woman suffrage movement itself had been split wide open on the Negro issue, and had developed an anti-Negro wing, of which Mrs. Catt, whether she realized it or not, became the inheritor. It was this tendency in Mrs. Catt's own movement which, twenty years after the franchise was granted to all women, she still reflected and tried to pass on to me.

I am not primarily concerned with what Mrs. Catt's reaction was then or is now. Mrs. Catt has performed a tremendous service for the nation in her suffrage work, and I, as all others, will honor that. But I offer her reaction about Negro leadership only as an example of how so many Americans have failed in their understanding, information, obligation, and attitude toward the Negro. Most presidents of the United States have been no clearer on this issue than was Mrs. Catt, and a few have been deliberately unconcerned. Most cabinet members since 1876 have understood this no better than the presidents and Mrs. Catt. United States Supreme Court justices have struggled with the political, economic, and moral issues involved and emerged with no greater strength than the others. I merely cite Mrs. Catt as another example of the traditional attitude which, like a roadside marker, notes the course our nation has traveled: to Hades, the Hades of the Civil War, and to potential hells of new conflict in the future.

The facts are these.

Just as, in general, organized labor can be said to lead the Negro, or to be the centrifugal force around which Negro advancement is now circling, there is a corresponding Negro leadership which is intimately involved in this process. The effect of Negro leaders in their own communities and organizations is largely determined by the depth of their connection with organized labor. It can often be said that they are followed by Negroes to the extent that they have the confidence and following of labor. He who leads the Negro toward integration with white labor carries weight in the Negro community. Thus there operates a reciprocal involutionary process of Negro labor leadership affecting both Negro and white.

One could list scores of Negroes now making a serious impact on the Negro communities and the broad American scene. But this is not a Who's Who nor an achievement record, and I speak of certain individuals only in so far as they are illustrative of movements, relationships, and processes in the white-Negro advancement pattern.

The attempt of the colored Man in the Street to find faith and direction in individual Negroes and the organizations they lead is a main concern. But no one Negro leads today in the same sense that, a century ago, Frederick Douglass was the outstanding political guide. Sometimes I suspect that "everybody wants to be Frederick Douglass," that is, to wear the mantle of leadership symbolized in the earlier prophetic era by Douglass. That is a worthy aspiration. I think that the figure who has most approximated Douglass since his death is W. E. B. DuBois. And I deliberately pass over Booker T. Washington, who held a dominant position while Douglass was still alive and throughout the early part of the present century.

Booker T. Washington was strictly a white man's Negro, rather than the Negro's choice. His conciliatory policy, coming at a time when a large portion of white America wanted the Negro to surrender much or most of his new freedom, won for him a great press build-up as *the* leader of the Negroes, and the Negro group found itself in the position of having a commander foisted upon it by the dominant group. What was ironic and tragic was that for several decades thereafter Negroes very largely followed Washington. Even to the bitter end, until this very day, Booker T. Washington is the choice of the supremacists of the nation as the ideal type of Negro leadership. This was rather bitterly proved in the recent period when his bust was placed in New York University's Hall of Fame. Washington received his place there after

Negroes had agitated for twenty years for Douglass' election. The educators who named Washington revealed in this selection not their friendliness toward the Negro, but their prejudice. They very deliberately ignored the incessant labors to get Douglass into the Hall, for Douglass was the symbol of the anti-slavery movement, whose memory white supremacy in our time still fears. When Richmond Barthé's bust of Washington was unveiled on the campus of New York University, Negroes welcomed the incident as another "first," but most Negroes and knowing whites understood that the real Negro great and immortal had been studiously by-passed.

Proof? When one enters the office of any Negro labor leader today it is the picture of Douglass that hangs on the wall, not that of Booker T. Washington.

The reign of Washington was shaken by W. E. B. DuBois, who challenged the compromise approach of the conciliator forty years ago. Since then DuBois has been a considerable influence. In his declining years he has been in charge of colonial research for the National Association for the Advancement of Colored People, and has helped make the Negro aware of his relationship to colonial peoples and to take pride in the African contribution to world culture. Recently DuBois went on the picket line of a telephone strike in New York, and soon afterward joined the staff of the *New Masses.* His main contact with the Negro at the moment is through the *Defender,* where his column appears above mine. Through this avenue he has been reaching hundreds of thousands of Negroes, influencing their understanding of world economic and political forces.

Although the role of labor in the life of the Negro has assumed great importance, it is by no means the whole story, and there are many other forces and individuals exerting effective leadership.

"You know, that's our big organization," said one informed Negro to me, describing the National Association for the Advancement of Colored People. That is true, of course, for the Association has about a half-million dues-paying members. A political arm of the Negro, taking up legal, social, economic, and civil-liberties issues of the colored people, the Association exerts great pressure upon many areas of white society and especially upon government. Its executive secretary, Walter White, has broad responsibility, and White, with the power of his organization behind him, has won numerous democratic advances.

What the Association does from day to day throughout the country is well symbolized in a lesser-known figure, James E. Allen, with offices in Harlem where he heads the Association's work in upper New York State. Not the public figure, nor the national symbol that White is, still Allen personifies the true spirit of the perennial NAACP man who grimly, seriously, incessantly functions like a "Jimmie Higgins" and more often than not passes from the scene without having received the plaudits or praises of either group. In Allen's case he was recently given a testimonial banquet for his years of service and leadership in the group. But my point, in singling him out, is merely to reveal that there are hundreds like him throughout the nation.

Another large Negro-based organization is the National Urban League, headed by Lester Granger, an experienced and effective individual who, like White, has a facility for penetrating white America and winning the confidence of influential whites. The League grew up because of the Great Migration. Its main object has been to secure immediate economic and cultural gains for the Negro. Fighting the battle of restrictive housing, placing people at jobs, putting pressure on white employers to open up their plants to Negroes, the NUL, with affiliates in fifty-three cities and three hundred and fifty full-time staff members, reaches about one-half of the urban Negro population. In the recent period one of the League's ablest representatives has been Dr. Alphonse Heningburg, a youthful, zealous, and highly articulate man formerly in charge of the organization's educational work.

The National Negro Congress, a convention movement which symbolizes the independent political fight of the Negro, embraces about three hundred Negro organizations. When its tenth-anniversary celebration occurred in Detroit in 1946 nearly one thousand leaders, mostly Negroes, from throughout the nation gathered and adopted a program to extend social justice for Negroes. That is a pretty good picture of the scope of Negro leadership: that one thousand leaders, representing several hundred organizations, could get together. The secretary of the Congress is Revels Cayton, who developed as a West Coast labor leader. There, in Cayton, confirmation again of the thesis that labor leads and symbolizes the Negro.

Paul Robeson, who has been called "the greatest personality of the age," moves Negroes but may have more impact upon whites. I think that Negro Americans have been a little slow to recognize the extent of Robeson's recognition by whites. His social-political contribution, perhaps more international in scope than that of any other Negro, complementing his artistic gifts, has won him a unique position. Mary McLeod Bethune, who heads the National Council of Negro Women, has a policy-making position of importance in many interracial organizations, and it is doubtful whether there is one Negro man in the nation who is more popular with the mass of the Negroes than is "Mother" Bethune. She was especially influential throughout the Roosevelt period. A. Philip Randolph's spadework with the Fair Employment Practices Committee movement and his labor leadership before then have won him an extensive hearing among Negroes, but his anti-Sovietism has limited his influence in the political sphere. This is not necessarily an effective technique among Negroes who are angrier with our own government than with any other. This is especially so in the face of the widespread understanding among Negroes that the Soviet Union is moving in the direction of harmonizing ethnic and national groups.

Father Divine's Peace Mission continues to influence thousands of Negroes and a large number of whites. Once, when I described in the *Defender* a Divine banquet in Newark, New Jersey, and treated both the banquet and the Peace Mission movement sympathetically, pointing out the economic advantages to its followers, I received a note from a Divine interpreter correcting me on one point: Father Divine was God, and I'd go further as a journalist if I realized it. I haven't yet realized that, but I can confirm Father Divine's steady fight against Hearst, all discrimination, and his respect for labor.

The influential Max Yergan, head of the Council on African Affairs, is widely admired for his role as a connecting link with the Negroes of other lands. The fact that Councilman Benjamin J. Davis, Jr. is a Communist seems in no way to have lessened his prestige among Negroes; he rates as a fighter. Percy Green, editor of the Jackson (Miss.) *Advocate,* is a power in his state. Doxey Wilkerson, economist and educator and editor of Harlem's *People's Voice,* is highly esteemed. J. Finley Wilson, fraternal organization leader of several hundred thousand Negro Elks, has an extensive influence and following. Channing Tobias, member of the executive board of the Y.M.C.A., has an important role as a liberal Republican. Champion Joe Louis packs a political punch that vies with his pugilistic dominance. Ferdinand Smith has for many years been a leader of the powerful National Maritime Union. A prominent Southern leader is Osceola McKaine, publisher of the Charleston *News and Observer* and chairman of the South Carolina Progressive Democratic Party. There are perhaps a dozen Negro councilmen in various cities of the nation.

Leadership seems mainly to be in the hands of men, but women are often the backbone of the protest and organization movements. Artists like Lena Horne, Pearl Primus, and Hazel Scott speak out on social issues. Mrs. Charlotte Bass gives militant editorship to her West Coast paper, the *California Eagle*. Charlotte Hawkins Brown is a Southern educator of prominence. Mrs. Anna Arnold Hedgeman has labored intensively for Fair Employment Practices

Committee legislation. In New York Audley Moore and Claudia Jones, Communist spokeswomen, have been fighting Harlem's battles for the last ten years. Thelma Dale of the National Negro Congress is a youthful contributor of talent. Gwendolyn Bennett, once a poet, founded and directs one of Harlem's most valuable institutions, the George Washington Carver School, and she takes part in the community's political life.

In the origins of America the Negro church may have provided the principal source of Negro leadership. Again history explains this, for, in the early life of the slave, there was no press, no effective means of communication, and no organization was allowed. Slave groups had to meet secretly or not at all. They had "cells" on their plantations where they might discuss escape or revolt. The group's constriction was complete. There was only one flaw in the system of the imprisoning class. White America slowly allowed "Christianity" to come to the Negro. It permitted the Negro to use the Bible, to have Sunday meetings, to develop a preacher class. Yet this very process helped in the undoing of the plantation owners and the slave traders. The Negroes turned their church gatherings into protest meetings. They studied the Bible with a view to finding in it that which would sustain their right to deliver themselves. And they did find plenty to quote, plenty with which to torment the conscience of their owners. In the main, the enslaving class tried to use religion to make the Negro suppliant, but the Negro penetrated this purpose, and religious revolutionaries like Nat Turner and Denmark Vesey and others appeared. The men who led the revolts justified them on the basis of religious and Christian right. In the anti-slavery period the Old Testament became a virtual arsenal of ammunition for the Negro and his white allies. Frederick Douglass once remarked that he intended to continue "making drafts on the Bible" to use in the struggle against slavery.

During the last two or three generations there has also been a

[196

trend in Negro life to allow religion, the church, and Christianity to dull the political protest of the Negro. In many areas of the Negro church the old revolutionary implications of "an eye for an eye and a tooth for a tooth" began to disappear, and the "turn the other cheek" element of the religious spirit projected itself. As new forces and individuals came into Negro community life, Negroes turned away from churchmen for leadership and looked to a rising class of newspaper editors and publishers, business people, labor leaders. And the preachers had to tie up with this new leadership by supporting them, or themselves become publishers or labor men.

Probably the best example of how these two trends have met in one individual is in the story of Congressman Adam Clayton Powell. Powell inherited his Baptist church; but his church was always a protest force, a meeting place, a political center as much as a religious institution. Then he turned publisher of the *People's Voice,* became a crusading preacher-editor-political independent. Here was the crystallization, in one individual and force, of several currents historically at work in the Negro community. It was this combination of factors, being pastor of a large political-religious grouping, and editor of a protest and interracial welfare paper, together with receiving labor support that won him at last a Congressional seat.

The chance of any Negro preacher getting the endorsement of the Negro community right now and being elected to office is pretty slight unless that minister is, in the first place, a fighter and demonstrator. All of this is evidence of the great common sense of the Negro community, of its insistence that it will not be fooled, that it knows what it wants and whom it wants.

Probably the Negro press is the greatest single idea-making force in Negro life at the moment. It chances that several of the big-circulation Negro newspapers remain tied to the Republican Party in a period when most Negro voters in the North have moved over to the New Deal or liberal-PAC wing of the Democratic

Party. The Pittsburgh *Courier,* the Baltimore *Afro-American,* and the New York *Amsterdam News* are examples of this affixation to the Republican Party even though there is no longer much to differentiate on Negro issues between the Republican Party and those Southern Bourbon Democrats always being attacked by the Negro press. Other influential papers who lead their readership, at least right now, along with the Democratic, labor, and sometimes left candidates are the Louisville *Defender,* the Oklahoma *Black Dispatch,* the Chicago *Defender,* and Ludlow Werner's traditionally Republican *New York Age.*

The information and the truth denied the Negro people in the white press, radio, movies, public-school system, and other mediums of communication, filter through to them in their press. It is a press, by and large, that informs, educates, protests, and corrects; therefore, to a considerable extent, it leads.

Finally, the Negro's struggle for integration will, I think, project to the very fore of labor more than one Negro in the coming period. In America the true "proletariat" is the Negro, living on a level far more basic to the nation's economy than even that of the white worker. The logic of a slave base drove Frederick Douglass, in the anti-slavery period, to a militancy and clarity that secured for him the theoretical and practical overseership of the entire abolitionist movement. It is an interesting precedent for similar possibilities in the ranks of labor today.

CHAPTER SIXTEEN

GRADUALISM VERSUS IMMEDIACY

A LIBERAL white acquaintance and a Negro woman were discussing in my presence the question of whether Negro liberation would come soon or late, and the white woman said: "Personally I don't think the Negro will be fully delivered from his social condition until there is a complete amalgamation of colored and white. That might take several hundred years." The colored woman looked at the back of her hand, which was brown, and remarked, "You mean I've got to wait until my hand gets white?"

There isn't much consolation for Negroes in being told that time will assuage their wounds and that it will also correct white attitudes and practices. The situation reminds me of the childish message I saw chalked up on a building in my neighborhood, "You was here and I wasn't, now I'm here and you wasn't." Time and tense may be a matter of no great importance in the realm of children's play, but in the brutal world of adulthood it is well to have both the tenses and the facts as straight as possible.

One of the numerous myths in wide circulation holds that Negroes are patient, quiet, and submissive. Along with this belief goes the conception held by some of the "best-regulated liberals" that the Negro is willing to slide along with things as they are. Nothing could be further from the truth, as the whole record of militance and revolutionary endeavor of the Negro attests.

Allan Nevins expressed this attitude. "I think the Negro should be a little patient," the Columbian historian told me. "Patience has been one of his greatest virtues."

Yet if someone were to step on the toes of Nevins' left foot, and press down hard, I am sure that that gentleman and scholar would urge him to get off immediately; and might possibly kick the offender's shins with his free foot.

When Nevins tried to tell me of the Negro's patience, he revealed that he either didn't know or didn't care to know of the hundreds of slave revolts in American history, that he was blind to or undisturbed by the intergroup clashes and political demonstrations of our own day, oblivious to the protest meetings, conventions, and interracial gatherings in process daily throughout the country. He was unaware, for a man who has been in politics, of what Representative Rankin, Senator Bilbo, and all others in Congress have been very much aware of—that the Negro has no room for the word "patience" in his thinking, speaking, or practice.

Hans V. Kaltenborn, the elderly but highly articulate radio commentator, who likes to appear as a liberal, was frightened at the thought of swift action by anyone in the Negro's behalf. When I suggested that the Negro is out for full integration, he suggested the possibility of resultant violence should the Negro press his case too intensively. "That would be my ideal," he said, "but I realize it's only an ideal. The more he demands it, the more he is likely to slow up his achievement. You always stir up a kick-back when you put a thing too strongly. Put it more quietly, you wouldn't stir up all that reaction and perhaps you could make more steady progress."

It was most revealing too that Mr. Kaltenborn believed that the Negro did not need to train more lawyers, orators, and politicians. The Negro has enough of these, he said, but what he needs is more farmers, skilled artisans, and teachers.

I was grateful for Kaltenborn's candor. There is nothing more useful to an aspiring group and its allies than to see clearly the strategy of one's adversary. Here was a candid admission that the political advance of the Negro is objectionable. Surely Kaltenborn knows that it is from the legal group that the nation recruits most of its Congressmen, cabinet members, city and state officials. Kaltenborn doesn't want to see the Negro in positions of authority, and obliquely says so. It is lawyers who become politicians and orators, so let us not have any Negro lawyers.

But the Negro knows that he needs lawyers. He needs thirteen millions of them. As a person of color once put it to me, "Every Negro is a spokesman for the group." This means that the more articulate each Negro becomes, the more rapid will be the group's progress.

Congresswoman Clare Boothe Luce hinted at the same possibility of violent repercussions against the Negro if he and his allies moved too swiftly. She did not feel that the question whether liberation came soon or later was the important one. "It should come about as rapidly as is possible without provoking a reaction of a violent nature," she said. "The rate of change in the Negro-white situation must be related to the rate of change in our industrial and economic life. I think the Negro has a right to demand 'immediate rights' as often and as loudly as he chooses within the framework of law. Personally I think that change in the Negro-white situation will come about gradually. It has taken seventy years to get it where it is now. It may take another fifty before the Negro is fully integrated into our system."

So much is wrong with the Luce statement and it is such a typical liberal misconception that it would demand a detailed analysis if space were here available. Answering it succinctly, I would say this: The threat of a reaction is not especially frightening to people already living in a chronic state of national and historical reaction. Change in the Negro status cannot wait for the vague promise held out in "the rate of change in our industrial and economic life." This has little persuasion, for it requests the Negro to trust to the good intentions of a government run primarily by the South, and to an economic future based on an "American Century" program as opposed to the "Century of the Common Man" idea in which the Negro more deeply believes. As to Mrs. Luce's charitable acknowledgment of the Negro's right to protest as loudly as he wants to "within the framework of law," the Negro still rates as outside the Constitution. He is therefore compelled to find different tools from the ones prescribed by those who deny their use to the Negro. Finally, when Mrs. Luce says that it has taken seventy years for the Negro to get where he is now, all that she is saying is that it has taken white America seventy years to evolve the present form of its rigid caste-economic system. She assumes this to be a positive advance whereas, actually, it may well be a status fully as malignant, albeit more subtle, than chattel slavery.

My reason for recording this dimness in such public lights as Hans Kaltenborn and Clare Luce is to indicate that theirs are typical and widespread attitudes. They are the views that issue from so very many individuals in public life, in financial and economic spheres, often in the arts, and usually in major party politics.

I would be reporting negatively if I failed to indicate that there are a great many individuals in responsible and influential positions who have much more clarity. For example, Marshall Field told me that he had a great sense of immediacy on the whole matter. "You can't approach it too quickly to please me," he said. Then there is Walter S. Mack, head of the Pepsi-Cola Company, who makes sure that his plant employs Negroes on a fully representative basis in each department. He believes that the solution is going to take time, but he was willing to put it a little angrily to me, this way: "Nobody is doing all that he or she could do, because if white America pitched in properly we wouldn't have 'the problem.' There's a lot of conversation about it, but not enough action. Not many industrialists are conscious of their obligations either." Mack, who is just as fearful as Luce and Kaltenborn of a militant drive of the Negro and his white allies, takes the social-democratic po-

[202

sition that free enterprise and government ought to spend money freely "to make the necessary social changes."

I debated the issue, "Should Negroes Accept Jim Crow Hospitals," with John Temple Graves, white editor of the Birmingham *Age-Herald,* and Frederick D. Patterson, Negro president of Tuskegee Institute, in a three-way symposium in *Negro Digest.* Partly involved in this topic was the issue of early or later settlement of the question. Graves and Patterson argued that segregated hospitals were acceptable, while I said no. The editor contended the Negro should accept Jim Crow while building up good will among whites. The educator said substantially the same thing, adding that this had been the historical course of the Negro in the past and there was no reason for change now. My contrary position lay in the belief that we were living in a period of accelerated development of political events. We now had a powerful Negro voting bloc which did not exist a generation ago. Today's great labor movement advocating justice for the person of color was unknown as recently as 1930. America had also grown conscious of the role of the racist principle in our national life as a result of having fought against the same thing abroad. These developments had brought the Negro question to the fore in the United States, and history and experience were inclined toward immediate answers. This was a time for demanding the full loaf, for challenging the weaknesses and hesitations of the past. To advocate acceptance of new Jim Crow institutions today in any form anywhere was preparation for acceptance of such forms tomorrow, and twenty-five years later, and perhaps forever.

There can be no compromise with the question of when integration is to be achieved. We must assume, as the Garrisonians assumed a century ago: *Immediate Emancipation.*

Early Virginia law indicates a brief struggle to achieve a slave status for imported Africans. There could not have been more than a few thousands in the country by 1650, yet by 1660 we find the laws referring to them as slaves. It had taken no longer than a decade or two for the colonial leaders to fasten clamps on the people of color. No hesitation there, no dickering around with gradual enslavement. This same process of receiving slaves and swiftly enveloping them in a bonded status continued from that time forward until the abolition of the slave trade in 1808. Always the procedure was comparable to that of modern storm troops swooping down on an individual, arresting him, and placing him in jail. The enslavement process was just as swift and warlike as were the military raids on Africa in which the blacks were made captive.

While the enslavers of men have always moved swiftly, even militarily, the advocates of freedom have too often been swamped in the slough of gradualism. Our whole national history illustrates this, and it may be that we are saddled with Jim Crow largely because of this weakness. In the pre-Revolutionary War years the Quaker, Anthony Benezet, projected the idea of abolition of slavery. Benjamin Franklin added his voice. But the Quaker movement did not carry enough weight to prevent the growth of slavery. The principal weakness was the conciliatory action of the Founding Fathers themselves. The authors of the Constitution asked for abolition of the slave trade in 1808, a generation after the Constitutional Convention. The effect of this compromise with slavery lingers with us until this day. The action was gradualist procrastination that did America irreparable injury and paved the way for the Civil War. From 1787 through 1830 "the Negro question" was siphoned into the nation's economic bloodstream, made part of our morals, our law, our organic structure. Slaves were poured into the land in such droves around the turn of the nineteenth century and such a corresponding legal structure was erected to defend their bondage, that not even the cleansing action of the Civil War was able to eradicate from our social practice and thinking the habits of the slave period. When that period of national crime gave way to the anti-slavery agitation of the 1830's and 1840's, only then did the nation realize how deeply it had

[204

permitted itself to run backward. This nation, founded by people seeking freedom, a freedom fought for by thirteen colonies opposed to tyranny, had become, only one generation after that struggle, the harborer of the most shameless tyranny in world history.

In Benjamin Franklin's speech to the Constitutional Convention accepting the Constitution as the best possible document for that hour, he declared that weaknesses were inevitable in an agreement drawn up by such an assemblage of men "with all their prejudices, passions, their errors of opinion, their local interests and their selfish views." Franklin, who had inveighed against slavery, understood the slave-trade compromise in the Constitution for the evil that it was. His prediction that the Constitution would become the major claim of despotism became verified perhaps sooner than he suspected. It came in the form of the slave power's domination of the capital, its protection of slavery, and its struggle to spread slavery throughout the West and the North. Then came the anti-slavers, the Civil War, the Reconstruction, and to this day there remains as of old a system of Coventry for the same one-tenth of the nation. Compromise originating as a principle in the Constitution has become an American habit, a costly one for all, and apparently the present is a new period of people's payment. For three hundred years the Negro has lived figuratively two miles underground in a mine called the Constitution. At the entrance of the mine stands a guard named Compromise.

In 1833 Garrison saw the evil of compromise in the Constitution and called for "Immediate Emancipation." He declared the Constitution to be "a covenant with the devil." There was much truth in his utterance. His mistake may have been in the policy that he settled upon as a result of his interpretation. He called for dissolution of the Union, rather than for an amendment to the Constitution which was advocated by others and which, historically, followed. Right or wrong in his approach (and I believe his disunion theory was wrong), he helped open a new period for the testing of men and ideas. He and a phalanx of white and Negro allies demanded that the great evil of slavery be ended at once, and he preferred a sundered nation with a free North rather than a united one preserving slavery. Even then there were less concerned individuals and groups who said, as some do now, "Slow down, be gradual, it will straighten out in time, be careful of the reaction." While some gradualists were talking that way, in the South John C. Calhoun, theoretical spokesman for slavery, called the institution right, true, and inevitable, and he pressed for the most immediate and ruthless means for preserving it. With his biting reactionary drive he ground to bits emancipationists both North and South. He threatened secession and he meant it. His region did secede, and fought to the death. Was there gradualist compromise in that policy?

Again after the Civil War, the Confederate interest and its Copperhead friends in the North moved swiftly, not gradually, to restore white rule and Negro serfdom. Here was no mild moderatism, no quietism, nothing whatever but a wave of Reconstruction lynchings, the rise of the violent Klan, and the military seizure of the capitol buildings in one state after another. But that reaction had assistance from the nation's gradualists. National hesitation and compromise at the time helped turn the Negro back to the traditional enslaving group. And to this day the shadow of the slave power and its compromising allies still hangs over most of America and all Negroes. The decisive Southerners have always been those who believed in violent suppression and no compromise with ideas of Negro liberation. The liberals in the South have never been decisive because they have rarely shown a disposition to make the full demands which the situation requires, and in our own day Southern liberals too often join with Southern Bourbons in telling Northern progressives: "Stay out of the South. We'll settle it." While quietists and moderates make their snail's-pace gains, the neo-Confederates wait for the right situation to smash down heavily with their swift military blows that dash to bits the gentle talk and gentle action of the gradualists.

The lesson in all this should be implicit. Gradualist proposals can make little headway with an adversary whose weapon is to smash back violently at decisive moments. Long-term objectives such as freedom fifty or a hundred years from now are discarded by the South's tradition of swift, merciless blows restoring full white rule. There is every precedent in American history for believing that neo-Confederate rule in the South might attempt in our own time to expropriate the entire Negro group of all the property it has slowly acquired.

Economically the enslavement of the people of color has already cost the nation one civil war. It compels the South to have to buy two of everything, two schools, two toilets, two communities, two worlds. It enables realtors throughout the nation to exact higher rentals from the mass of whites for the dubious privilege of feeling prejudiced.

Morally, Jim Crow hasn't a leg to stand upon and I refuse to even discuss it morally.

The Jews, that classic yardstick for the measurement of all social questions, have been fighting for equality and justice for thousands of years. Yet nazism and its philosophy of immediate suppression took all of the freedom that the Jew had laboriously secured and wiped it out in less than ten years. Small chance would the Jews have in our struggling world if they said they would be willing to take justice as some vague handout on some vague distant day in some vague distant clime. About as much of a chance as the Negro would have if he were to say to himself or anyone else that he is willing to wait for some other generation to realize full freedom.

The white man, wondering what he is up against when he faces the question of how to get rid of the Jim Crow institution in America, should note carefully a statement made by a Southern editor, Floyd Tillery, writing in *Newspaperman*. Discussing what the South thinks of the Negro, he said, "For, in the South—yesterday, today and tomorrow—white is white and black is black, and 'Ne'er the twain shall meet' (in social relationships) though God himself should decree it from His Great Judgment Seat." Apparently, as some supremacists view it, if God Himself were black He'd be a Nigger too.

I do not mean, by arguing all this, to dissuade the liberals from doing whatever constructive work they are doing. I mean only to prod them and hurry them up. I would say as Frederick Douglass said about John Brown's march on Harper's Ferry: "The tools to those who can use them. Let every man work for the abolition of slavery in his own way. I would help all and hinder none." But it is the immediatists who are in the van to spur or isolate the hush-hush crowd, to clarify the gradualists, to win to their side all those of good will, and hasten up *all* liberation approaches.

These questions present themselves: Can the advocates of abolition of Jim Crow take gradualist and quietist positions when the proponents of group subjection have always been immediatists of the most militant order? How well does the "Go slow, don't incite reaction" approach hold up in the light of history? Does American experience validate any of those claims that a later generation will present us with equal relationships? If white supremacy moves with speed is it not a converse necessity for the Negro and his ally to counter-project the same instantaneity?

CHAPTER SEVENTEEN

THE AFRICAN HERITAGE

WHEN I was a boy this was Africa to me. . . .
The lions roared and the "natives" danced in fierce heat, the rain came down in buckets, snakes wrapped themselves around your neck the minute you got into the jungle, and the equator was a line you could snip in two with scissors. You could hear tom-toms everywhere as the cannibals came toward you, and you wondered how you would taste boiled up, with yams on the side and sprinkled with plenty of paprika. The big ants crawled around everywhere; there were mosquitoes and crocodiles, beating drums and elephants. You hacked your way through a jungle thicket, and spears would be flying at you while the animals sneaked around behind and jumped at you from the branches of the palms. The natives were constantly letting out bloodcurdling calls while the old drumbeats echoed steadily, and it was like that all over Africa except in Egypt. There they had a Pyramid.

Now the odd part is that when I go to the moving pictures today this is still the Africa that is presented to me. Once my visualization of Africa came from a few books, the things I heard at home and in school, and it was all cloaked with a special set of words: native, heathen, primitive, barbarian, infidel, mumbo jumbo, and missionary. Now I get the same picture of Africa from a series of "Zombie" pictures. Zombie pictures are supposed to be concerned with the West Indies and South America, but

209]

we are to understand that this goes for Africa too. Or else one of those "Bring Them Back Alive" pictures carries on the tradition. Frank Buck and the Martin Johnsons did their bit to further the exclusively wild-animal, wild-human approach to Africa and the tropic islands. The oddities in carnivals and circuses completed the picture.

Not unless one subscribes to a small four-page monthly circular called *New Africa* put out by the Council on African Affairs, or picks up a book like *My Africa* by Mbonu Ojike, will he learn that about one hundred and fifty million Africans are mainly *workers,* employed by a half-dozen or so occupying European countries, Britain, France, Belgium, Holland, Portugal, Italy, Spain, and even the United States. Not unless one gets a map of Africa with all these European countries stamped upon it, and then looks deeply into recent African history, will one find that Africa has been for centuries the labor reservoir of the West. Not unless one sees moving pictures of a city like Johannesburg does one know that the masses of Africans move through city streets, toil in mines, work the fields, live on special reservations, and hold on their backs, literally, a handful of parasitic foreign whites. Not unless one was aware of the fact would one know that "primitive" Africa is little more than a fictionist's dream and that real Africa is a chained mass of blacks straining at the leash and looking for the day when it will "throw all the foreigners out." Not unless one forges deeply into Negro American life will one learn how extensively the darker brother is ideologically tied to the people of Africa and other continents. And in examining the whole pattern of modern white-Negro, or European-African relations, the answer is to be found, not in looking at the Negro, nor even Africa, but at the white man and Europe and at what these have done to a continent and a people.

Broil a T-bone steak one-inch thick and eat it for your evening meal: does it play an important part in your life for that day?

Such is the part Africa plays toward Europe and the Western Hemisphere in modern times.

The Western world has been so busy taking golden eggs out of Africa for the past three or four hundred years that it has shown little interest in the age-old background of that continent. A few missionaries, a few explorers, a few students have plummeted the depth of Africa for something other than diamonds and gold, and they have come up with ancient cultures, with the belief that the origins of West African culture may go back twenty-five thousand years. Our present calendar year of three hundred and sixty-five days had its origin in Africa in 4241 B. C., and it was at about the same time that iron smelting was invented by Africans. Much of the important history presaging the modern era was already being enacted in Egypt. Africa was then an adult world compared to the contemporary tribal life of forest-covered Europe whose animal-skin clothed tribes were living in caves. Dynasties came and went in Egypt for thousands of years before Christ, and they drew their strength from inner Africa. The peoples of Africa, millions of them, were able to live without a British policy, without the help of missionaries to "civilize" them. While the English lived in caves along the Thames, and the Indians of our continent subsisted in elementary fashion on the soil and from hunting, while the Teutons were only savage migrants with clubs and flint weapons, the African world had already evolved many diverse kingdoms, nations, empires, civilizations. There had been competitive and communal life, feudal and slave systems. Around 900 A. D. there were great nations spread across the center of Africa, from coast to coast, nations with a total population of nearly eighty millions. There were the Yoruba, Ibo, Efik, Congo, with elaborate agrarian cultures; and prior to these the spreading and wealthy Songhai empire in western Sudan. Around 1300 A. D. flowered the Mandingo empire whose African art can be compared to Western Hemisphere achievements of today. Perhaps the outstanding cultural factor through the milleniums was the African village system,

211]

under which people lived with each other in relative amiability and cooperative effort at a time when Europe had no definite forms of collective living. But there has never been any solidly African culture or continent or unity. Modes of living have ranged from advanced cultures to such tribal and primitive civilizations as one might have found in Germany or Britain two thousand years ago.

When I asked Allan Nevins what he thought about the cultures of Africa as compared with those of Europe at the time when the Europeans prostrated the former continent with the slave trade, he answered, "You are comparing the worst of Europe with the best of Africa." But I was not. I was comparing two cultures, two worlds, two diverse moral, social, and economic environments.

Philosophers may compare "backward" Africa of the Sudanese period (when Europe was passing through the Middle Ages) with "forward" England of the modern colonial policy, or with Nazi Germany of 1939, or with the United States of 1947 playing atomic power politics. My position was best expressed in the statement made by an Iroquois Indian chief at Onondaga Reservation, near Syracuse, when we were fighting nazism. The Iroquois were observing an annual ceremony in which the federal government according to the terms of an agreement made one hundred and fifty years ago, made them a yearly gift of a few yards of cloth as payment for much of upper New York State. Said the Indian chief: "We Indians were a civilized people with a savage veneer. Then came your white culture, a savage people with a civilized veneer." He pointed to the Nazi holocaust in Europe to prove his point and impliedly he pointed to all Western competitive civilization.

Africa has been a jungle of animals, torrid heat, naked people, and great lakes, but it has never sent out missionaries to spread gospel with one book while in another they wrote down descriptions of a region's raw materials. There was no steel age in Africa in the year 1500 A. D., nor was there in Europe, but there was an agrarian economy on many parts of the continent more advanced than the ox economy of Europe. If people did not widely read in Africa in the year 1400, before Gutenberg, neither did they read widely in Europe before Gutenberg. If Europe had learned of gunpowder from the Chinese in the early part of the present millenium, the Africans had long since used gold—for ornaments, and not for wrecking empires.

There were tribes that lived in lost and remote areas of the African continent and they lived as close to the soil as the animals about them but they lived, and they had their codes, they enjoyed life in their own ways, and they were not ranged opposite each other in huge, menacing cultures suffering from the neuroses of metropolitan congestion and competitive struggle. They did have their economic struggles and understood them as such. When they had troubles over boundaries or properties they fought, and killed each other, but they did not do these things as the so-called civilized nations of the world have been doing them for centuries, in the name of saving souls, or for "democracy," "ideals," "civilization," or any of the other hypnoses that clothe international power politics.

With the year 1415 came the beginnings of the slave trade and of the steady looting and prostrating of this ancient continent and ancient people. It has been estimated that during the sixteenth, seventeenth, and eighteenth centuries fifty to a hundred million Africans lost their lives in the slave trade. About four out of five died in the resistance to enslavement. Perhaps fifteen millions arrived in the Western Hemisphere. Expatriate and destroy nearly a hundred million young people of one continent during three centuries and there is the blueprint for spoliation. Smash a continent to smithereens in order to build an empire on which the sun never sets and there is the key to modern world wars, the concept of imperialism, the twentieth-century issue now shaping up: *colonial freedom versus imperialism*. Compare the slaughter of six million Jews in Europe in ten years by the Nazis, and the slaughter and enslavement of ninety million Africans, principally by Britain

213]

and our own colonial forebears, and one finds the same modern logic in each action, the same press of empire, the same enrichment of one society at the expense of another, the same policy of totally expropriating a defenseless group. When one thinks of Christianity in modern times, one must remember that when Sir John Hawkins in 1652 captained the first English slave ship to Africa his vessel—carrying the seeds of contemporary Jim Crow—was named "The Jesus."

In 1792 Liverpool employed one hundred and thirty-two slave ships and the city itself had a very respectable class which benefited thereby and was influential in the formulation of empire policy. In America the Puritan wealth of Newport, Rhode Island, was being amassed from the same trade. The looting of Africa by means of bayonets, baubles, and Bibles was becoming the "key" to the "rise" of the Western Hemisphere. Britain fought two wars with Holland over rights to the slave trade and finally got control of the traffic between Africa and the British West Indies and between Africa and Spanish America. It was very much owing to the wealth of her African spoil, that England had the strength to complete her control and occupation of India begun around 1600. When England finally obtained all that was to be had from the slave trade, and when the conscience of the world became aroused against it, she "liberally" abandoned the traffic.

Left, right! Left, right! Left, right!

That is the Anglo-Saxon culture marching. It is the white peoples of Europe and the New World marching over the ravaged body of Africa. It is the year 1600. Then 1700. 1800. At last 1900. Still the white storm troopers with gunpowder in the right hand, whiskey and trinkets in a suitcase, a Bible under the left arm, a book of parliamentary procedure hidden under the hat, march through Nigeria, the Sudan, the Ashantee country, the Congo, South Africa. Four centuries of dishonor. Four centuries of the rape of a continent by a people many of whom mentally shout "Rape" at any Negro walking silently in the street. Ninety million

[214

African lives lost in order to build what?—to build the colonial estates of the American slave period, to till the soil westward to Texas until the present day, to fill the cotton mills of England with raw material for centuries and clothe a part of the world, to fill the pipes of men who smoke tobacco all over the West, to cultivate the coffee plantations and banana groves of South America for centuries. Europeans and Americans have been living off the loot of Africa and the bodies of brown- and black-skinned peoples, and still are. We in the United States are living on the cocoa, fruits, rubber, and manifold mineral imports of South America labored by people of black, brown, and red complexions. We taste the sweetness of sugar from the West Indies nurtured by blacks. We breakfast daily on the agrarian products of Negro Americans. We live under the folds of American flags made of cotton raised by black labor in the Southern states.

Again the image of the coin: African loot the one side, the British Empire and the threatening "American Century" the other; and thus Africa becomes a causal factor of paramount importance in the present world political conflict. American interests in Africa are not so extensive, one may argue: so what have the Africans against us? This: the logic of a colonial world which includes the "colored" of the world places the United States in the African's anti-imperialist outlook. Our past is catching up with us. The slave that was deposited on our shore by the British and transformed into a laboring tool by the colonial planters and is still Jim Crowed to the benefit of American economy is clasping hands with the West Indian, the African, the East Indian, the Latin American— and perhaps the Russian. The retiary world influence of Africa, historic objective of European conquest, has strands drawing back to itself whatever was once African and whatever is new, liberal, and in colonial interest. Africa, cut up in 1814 like a great hunk of steak and partitioned by Portugal, France, Britain, Spain, Holland, Denmark, and Turkey, stands as a force opposed to European and American conquest and exploitation. As Africa opposes the Euro-

215]

pean world for its direct invasion, so it opposes equally the United States which robbed Africa of its people and still uses them in both Americas as burden-carriers of national wealth.

When Madame Eugenie E. Eboue was elected deputy to the French Constituent Assembly from Guadeloupe she came to the United States before going to France, and I attended her press conference. A Protestant woman missionary asked her how America might help out in French Africa. "Can we help by advancing educational, religious, or cultural institutions?" the missionary asked, and then, after pausing an instant, she added, "Or by free trade?" Madame Eboue replied that the Africans knew what American customs were toward black-skinned people, and informed her bluntly that French Africans wouldn't be interested.

American customs toward the black-skinned here, or British customs toward the blacks in South Africa: Where and how can one make a choice? After four centuries of "civilizing the heathen," what, for example, have the British accomplished?

I talked with Stuart Cloete, the author of a number of books about South Africa. At the time he was standing in his modest penthouse in midtown Manhattan, erect, righteous, and liberal, as he said, "I am against segregation in Africa."

I suppose the pundits would refer to that as the height of something or other, possibly generosity. I do not mean to be disparaging. Cloete *was* being liberal, but at the moment his utterance shone a full light on one of the more obvious ironies of our time. One hundred and fifty million blacks live in Africa, and a handful of whites control them, yet a man finds himself in the spot, or history finds itself in such a spot, where the return of a continent to the people who live there anyway has to be asserted in the form of a liberal sentiment!

Under both the recent Tory Government and the current "socialist" British Labor Party, there exists such a legalization of prejudices in the Union of South Africa that, according to James B. Leyburn, professor of sociology at Yale University, "There is

[216

much evidence to support the contention that discrimination against the blacks in the Union of South Africa is more far-reaching, more cynical than in any other self-governing country in the modern world." South Africa's Land Acts limit the areas where Africans can reside, and restrict their ownership or disposal of property. The Color Bar Act prevents them from working in skilled occupations. Their trade unions are denied legal recognition. Special taxes are applied to Africans although they do not have representation. Finally, the Pass Laws require an African to carry as many as twelve different legal documents, under penalty of arrest for being any place where "he has no right to be." Hitler did not attempt to do more. The "yellow card" system for prostitutes under the czar was much milder restrictive legislation than this whole code applied to eight million South African blacks by two million whites and the absentee British beneficiaries.

But the repeated partitions of the continent have given rise to contradictions through which the Africans have made advances. In the 1920's something like an intellectual revolution began. Student movements were organized. Pamphlets on internationalism passed from Tripoli to the Union of South Africa. In 1935 when Italy invaded Ethiopia all Africa was crystallized as an anti-fascist force, a force that would be helpful later to France when Pétain would give his country to Hitler. By 1940 African newspapers, political parties, schools, fraternal societies had arisen everywhere, under each flag, and with an underlying continental unity. Young Africans were coming to America and attending our schools. Meantime Marcus Garvey had helped make Negro Americans conscious of their rich African tradition. Africans heard of the "Back to Africa" movement and took note of it. If it meant nothing else it signified that an ancient tie was being reaffirmed; this would have repercussions in the later period of labor-political development. Many Negro Americans began to think and act in terms of their "color" alliance to 360,000,000 brown-skinned people

217]

of India, 450,000,000 yellow people of China, 100,000,000 brown people of the Philippines area, 120,000,000 Latin Americans of Negro, Indian, and Portuguese mingling, as well as 150,000,000 Africans. Countless incidents occurred. East Indian visitors to the United States addressed Harlem community gatherings. In Harlem the National Memorial Bookstore erected a huge sign which stood for years, saying, "Read About 600,000,000 Colored People." The internationally hard-pressed color groups began to read each other's press, get together at conventions, support one another politically. When one hundred and fifteen Indonesian seamen manning Dutch ships went on a thirty-day strike in Manhattan harbor in protest against carrying munitions to be used by the Dutch against the Indonesian people, Harlem housed them for the period of the strike. Paul Robeson for Negro Americans and Jawaharlal Nehru for the Indian Congress exchanged telegrams when the Council on African Affairs in Madison Square Garden demanded freedom for all colonials. When South African diamond workers went on strike they cabled for help to the Congress of Industrial Organizations, and the Negro press splattered the news across its front pages in banner lines. When certain East Indian journalists came to the United States on a news assignment, they first approached Negro Americans to get steered to sources and people. By the end of World War II color had become a factor in the struggle for world democracy. All the way from Chicago to Cuba, to Guatemala, to Brazil, to the Congo, the people who originated in Africa were using all modern means of communication to reconstruct their shattered traditions. In Harlem a Provisional World Council of Dominated Nations, composed of spokesmen of subjugated nations living in the United States, was organized to counterpoint the United Nations Security Council which was by-passing the colonial question. Perhaps the whole process reached its symbolical peak in the appeal to the Soviet Union of the Indonesian premier seeking aid in throwing off Dutch Imperialist oppression. That premier may have spoken for

[218]

more millions than those of Indonesia. I can report that he spoke for a large segment of Negro Americans. Color and colonialism were the chief ingredients of that appeal, ingredients which so much compose Negro America.

Here is a typical example of the kind of color reasoning I came upon among many Negroes during the war. I found that sympathetic feeling for Japan was very widespread. Where there was such emotion it was based on Japan's being a "colored" country, as a country that belonged to the world forces of the colored peoples. That yellow Japan destroyed much of yellow China did not seem to matter; the sympathizers with Japan saw not Japan's imperialism, but only the fact that at last a "colored people" had taken up arms against the white world. Is there anything unusual in this when, after all, scores of millions of whites in the United States also reason in terms of "white" and "black" where the Negro is concerned? Why should the Negro American think in color terms any less than white Americans when both have been subject to a color-oriented political, economic, and legal structure for three hundred years?

"You will have to admit," said one Negro to another, "that Japan has put our people ahead one hundred years." Another acquaintance, always sympathetic to the Soviet Union, was shocked when the Soviet declared war on Japan and said, "The Soviet knifed Japan in the back." My friend expected the Soviet as a champion of colonial and colored peoples to be on Japan's side. Here was, of course, a complete failure to recognize the economic forces at work internationally and failure to see the arisen Japan as a military-imperialist nation tied in with Western fascism.

I mention this deep-based color orientation of the Negro, stamped upon him for generations, to show his walled removal from the main stream of American life and to indicate the reason for the Negro's incessant questioning of, challenging of, and sometimes indifference to much of the nation's jingo nationalism and "American Century" thinking.

219]

I have never yet met a Negro so sold on the American democracy generally, so convinced of our "ideals" of profit and power and international prestige, so absorbed in what the Fourth of July orators call "our way of life" that he or she sounded like a rampant American nationalist. I have never yet heard a stump speech from a Negro glorifying the standard of living, and the morality abroad in the land, as I have heard all my life from business and church leaders and deliverers of baccalaureate addresses. That attitude just doesn't exist among Negroes. Negroes haven't felt it, or lived it. Always there is the arms akimbo attitude, the lifted eyebrow, the cocked, listening head to indicate a very natural skepticism and sense of criticism. No word is bandied about in America any more casually than the word "democracy," and the Negro would like to use the tradition of democratic advance to move ahead himself, but I have seen it spelled in the Negro press "demockracy." That is why Negro leaders have so often been over on the left, that is why their protest has been tinged with socialism or shot through with it.

Ever since Italy invaded Ethiopia the Negro American, the West Indians, and the Africans have had a clear understanding of fascism and have rejected it. When Hitler singled out Jews for special attack Negro Americans remarked, "That's what we have been experiencing for centuries." Negroes, therefore, found themselves organically in the camp of democracy in its struggle against fascism, but what bothered the Negroes, West Indians, and Africans was exactly what concerned the East Indians, Chinese, Middle Easterners, and Latin Americans: "The Allies are fighting a racist, fascist tyranny in Europe. Do they understand that they themselves have been protecting, fostering, and inculcating racism in their homelands and in the colonies? Will they turn and yield up the racism of which they are guilty themselves after defeating the racism and reaction of Hitler? Will America abandon Jim Crow? Will England give India its independence? Will the Dutch,

[220

fighting the Nazis, give up Indonesia? Will the French pull out of French Equatorial Africa?"

These were the questions which world Negroes, colonials, and "colored" asked themselves during World War II while in the main throwing their support to the Allies because they understood clearly that the most aggressive and dangerous racism had become Germany's. They knew that if Germany's racism triumphed such a victory would initiate the sternest racist occupation of the whole world since the time of the slave trade. They realized that Germany would introduce everywhere a repression exceeding even that of the British in South Africa. They comprehended that a Nazi Germany occupying America would make the fullest possible use of a Bilbo or a Rankin in the restoration of chattel slavery. The logic of democratic advance therefore threw the largest segment of the Negro population clearly on the side of the Allies in the struggle against the Axis, but Negroes, utilizing the world contradictions surrounding the question of "race," pressed their own issues with even greater sharpness than before the war and understood that at the close of the war the drive would have to continue with even greater ferocity.

Now the point of the intensified Negro pressure during and upon completion of the war is this: that the most farseeing elements in the Negro community appear to have taken a leftward turn.

Consider the position of Dr. Carter G. Woodson, the historian and founder of "Negro History Week," founder of the Association for the Study of Negro Life and History, publisher and traditional non-partisan leader of the Negro group. All his professional life he has been non-partisan, out of actual political parties, and he has never allowed the organization of which he is the head to become the instrument of any party. Yet in a recent discussion with me Dr. Woodson declared his belief that the world was going socialist, that the colonial peoples of the world were moving that way rapidly, and that Negro Americans had either great respect for or an attitude of neutrality toward the idea of world socialism. Finally, in his monthly periodical, the *Negro History Bulletin,* Woodson placed himself definitely in the camp of world labor and socialism. He foresaw the possibility in the near future of a Labor president, declared that the drive of labor was irrepressible, suggested that this was a highly salutary thing for the Negro, and asserted that a Labor president "will make possible the nationalization of industry—the elimination of the industrialists in order to secure democratic control of everything concerned with the production of food, shelter, fuel, and clothing and the lines of communication and transportation."

At about the same time Woodson was making this statement Dr. William S. Nelson, dean of Howard University's School of Religion, was saying that if socialism presented itself as a live possibility and choice "it would have predominant Negro support." He said: "The Negro is eating the crumbs of democracy. If, as can happen, socialism should become a choice, the Negro in light of his experience could not be counted upon to support the kind of democracy he knows." What is significant about Nelson's statement is that it comes from a Negro religious head, from the type of leadership which, in the past, caviled to supremacist demands. That day is now gone.

The books of Negro leaders which appeared at the close of World War II showed this trend. Walter White's *A Rising Wind* concluded with the intimation that if Anglo-Saxon practices in China and India were not drastically and immediately revised, it was probable and perhaps certain that the people of India, China, Burma, Malaya, and other parts of the Pacific might move into the Russian orbit. W. E. B. DuBois, dean of them all, put it more directly than any, saying: "Come what may, it is to the glory of God and the exaltation of man that the Soviet Union, first of modern nations, has dared to face front-forward the problem of poverty, and to place on the uncurbed power of concentrated wealth the blame of widespread and piteous penury."

[222

What am I reporting? My own views? Not necessarily. I am describing how a great mass of Negroes are thinking and where a significant and *leading* section of them is moving—fast. Am I warning anyone? Not at all. I am not interested in advising Mr. Bilbo how to save Mississippi's brand of "civilization," where the average annual income is $220 per person. White America has rejected Negro America, perhaps the largest single contributor to the national wealth and culture. White America has only itself to blame if the Negro keeps moving leftward. The Negro, I believe, takes the position that he has the right to look for salvation anywhere he can find it, and since our social system all the way from George Washington to Harry Truman hasn't provided the answers, there is more and more international thinking and action by this group. Right now I would say that the Garrisonian expression, "My country is the world, my countrymen all mankind," has much more concrete validity among Negro Americans than the pledge of allegiance. Nobody can be expected to have allegiance to chains. The Negro's allegiance right now, as I see it and am compelled to report it, is to labor, color, liberalism, colonial fraternity, "common man's" rights everywhere, the *idea* of democracy and a free America he fights for but has never known.

As for that eerie sound occasionally heard high up near the rafters in the British Parliament, that's the vulture of the slave trade come home to roost as the explosive colonial question. And what one sees atop the Capitol Building in Washington isn't the proud bald eagle. It's a crow, and cawing to beat hell too.

223]

CHAPTER EIGHTEEN

JIM CROW CROSSROADS

"Democracy is not simply the self-defense of the competent; it is the unloosing of the energies and the capabilities of the depressed."
—WILLIAM E. B. DUBOIS, in *Color and Democracy*.

HAVE I been harsh on the supremacists of the land? I think I have been no more severe with this segment of society than it is with itself. I have not been half so caustic as the racist is brutal to himself, his family, and his society. Nothing that I have said or ever could say could portray that wing of America as it has portrayed itself—as I shall forthwith show.

In August of 1946, when political tensions were high in Georgia and Governor Arnall faced the challenge of Eugene Talmadge's return to gubernatorial power, racist violence flared in Walton County, Georgia. Two Negro men and their wives were lynched near Monroe in a massacre that was a backdrop for the "white supremacy" issue which Talmadge had introduced into the campaign, and an outraged nation sprang into protest.

I received a telephone call from an old friend, Lawrence Gellert. He is a poetic figure who has spent twenty years in the South gathering folksongs: he has a thousand of them. He looks like a native Southerner and "passes" as such when he is there. He asked me to help him go South to investigate the Monroe lynchings, and so I arranged with the Civil Rights Congress for his dispatch to Georgia. He spent two weeks in the vicinity of Monroe posing as a cotton farmer desirous of buying cotton land. He listened to the comments on the lynching, and since his ears catch up folk talk and hold it there like a basin catching rain water, he came away with a unique record.

The Monroe postmaster told Gellert: "No, we don't hang no reward sign on our board here. This is federal property and the killing of those niggers is strictly the business of the state." A farmer explained it this way: "Whatever you grow got to be thinned out now and then. You raise you a better crop that way. Niggers is no different." A counterman theorized: "With January close by and Talmadge on his way back, none of them state investigators gonna turn in nobody. They'd get their fat ass kicked off the Bureau sure as God made little apples." A four-year-old was suspicious of Gellert and said, "I can't even say hello to you because my mamma said you never know who you're talking to." A bus station agent had this yarn: "A fancy tricked-up nigger asks for ticket to Monroe down in Atlanta. They sell it to him all right but phone me to have the police waiting for him here. Sure enough, when bus hits town one of them suitcase niggers with a three-dollar necktie and all steps right down into the arms of the chief of police. He was investigating the lynching of them four niggers. Had him a nerve all right. Chief of police asks him if he think niggers done it. And when he said he sure didn't think so, the chief asks him if he thought a nigger would be allowed to investigate white folks. And then he asks him if he wanted to stay a long time or would he be ready to leave right away. The nigger wasn't in town more'n five minutes." A respectable citizen discussed lynch justice: "These killings at the Appalachee were not lynchings, sir. Lynch law is justice we sometimes resort to in order to save time, expense, and possibly loopholes for the criminal. This was murder pure and simple and I'm sick and tired of hearing it dignified by any other name." And this, from a real-estate man, revealing the economic origin of lynching, segregation, and "race": "You want to buy some good cotton land? Grow you the best cotton in middle Georgia, sir, if you can get your sharecroppers right. And since that little nigger trouble we done had, maybe that shouldn't be hard now. And no raise of prices for the accommodation, either. Don't mind that. It's only a little joke of mine. But there are heaps of folks think their acres worth more since the niggers ain't gonna be so independent like they was."

Publisher John Sengstacke of the *Defender* became especially interested in the Walton County massacre, offering a large reward for information leading to conviction of the killers, and he asked me to fly to Georgia and look into the case. Before leaving I arranged with leaders of the National Citizens Political Action Committee, heads of several of the principal interracial organizations, and several Congressmen to carry to Governor Ellis Arnall, on an unofficial level, a message of concern for his political future owing to the situation in which he had been placed as a result of the lynchings. I had arranged this by telephone in New York with the Governor's aide, but when I arrived in Atlanta, Arnall and his office sedulously passed me up.

The newly nominated Eugene Talmadge was curious to meet a white man writing for a Negro paper, and he invited me to his room in the Henry Grady Hotel. I told him that the Atlanta Negroes had expressed great anxiety concerning his expected return to office, and that I should like to convey to them some expression from him allaying their fears. But Talmadge had no good word for them, or for the whole country. He at once attacked the Negroes' desire to vote as "nothing but communism" and said he would disfranchise them as soon as he could get action by the state legislature. "Only thing the nigger respects in a good spanking," he said. "That's the way to handle the nigger. Take him out in back of the barn and give him a good spanking. He'll love you for that. Finish with him and he'll say, 'Yassuh, boss,' and he likes it and you'll get along all right. This is a white man's country, Anglo-Saxon country and the niggers don't want to vote." He went on eloquently in a tradition which, I submit, has not gone with any wind. He wound up saying: "There's been enough talk. What we want now is *action, action.*"

A few hours later I talked with the Governor-nominate of Alabama, James E. Folsom. He made much more sense, revealed "the living South," the South of new hope and a dream of decency. He struck a different note. He told me that the biggest evil in his state was absentee ownership of industry. Most of the transportation, communication, mines, and steel industries of his state were Northern-owned, he pointed out. "In other words, sweat and dollars and cents are being drained out of the South." He would take issue with this situation, he promised, and encourage Southern financing of its own industry. I talked with Folsom about the possibility of Northern liberals' forming a political coalition with Southern liberals, a kind of under-bridge of progress that would oppose the old alignment of Northern and Southern conservatism. I said: "The people of the North and the South have been too long opposed. Yet the conservatives of both sections are in agreement and they work together in Congress. Why cannot liberals North and South, who will agree on some kind of minimum with respect to the Negro question, also close ranks, find a common strength?" He followed that line of thinking with interest.

I see a great political possibility in such a development. If it is true that the mass of working people in the North, the small business and farming groups, are under the domination of great interests—and it is true—and if the Southern farmer, sharecropper, small businessman, and even the bigger businessman of the South are also under the same Eastern financial-industrial control, then there should be a basis for common political accord between these forces. Big money splits the North away from the South, cuts off

227]

the Negro from the white, plays one group against the other. That has its logic.

It would be well for the "common man" and the liberals of all sections to try to find means of healing the traditional North-South schism—but not at the expense of the Negro—and to concentrate a joint fire at the industrial and financial giants who benefit from this age-old sectional split. There are great forces in the South now which understand that the Negro question cannot be compromised any longer, that the Negro must have economic justice, that the whole South cannot have progress until the Negro question is faced. They are willing to make some concessions. Folsom, for example, said he was going to make an all-out fight to rid Alabama of the poll tax during his administration. Men and women everywhere can welcome that and can welcome a strengthening of the bonds between the progressive North and the forward-moving South. When the Southern white man sees clearly that his real enemy is not the Negro, not organized labor, not the great mass of people of the North, but *absentee ownership,* then there will be progress.

I am in agreement with the thesis of A. G. Mezerik in his recent *Revolt of the South and West,* in which he sees the need of a South-West combination to fight "the corporate aristocracy" of the East. When the South concentrates its fire on Northern ownership instead of upon a group of agrarian workers in the main property-less, it will attain political maturity. When economic and social forces North, South, West, and East form a new political coalition to oppose the power of absentee Eastern investment, then the blight of white supremacy will at last be attacked from the proper direction. When free enterprise in the South and West start moving against Eastern monopoly, labor and the Negro people will join in that advance.

While in the South I secured information which confirms Mezerik's theory of Eastern financial domination of the South. I learned that it influences political reaction in the South as much as

[228

the productive forces of the region itself. Talmadge was aided extensively in his campaign by the practically wholly Northern-owned Georgia Power Company. Thomas L. Stokes, Pulitzer Prize columnist, in a New York *World-Telegram* dispatch of July 19, 1946, datelined from Atlanta, wrote: "An interesting story of political intrigue not new lies behind the victory of Eugene Talmadge here. It involves big financial and industrial interests, some with roots elsewhere, largely in the East. They knew what they wanted, they played for it, and they got it." Robert Roth, writing a series of articles for the Philadelphia *Record* in the summer and fall of 1946, made the same assertion, stating that Eastern money was behind Talmadge. And everywhere I went in Georgia, political actives who were on the inside repeated the refrain, "Big money from the North helped lick Ellis Arnall." Later I telephoned Thomas Stokes in New York to confirm his views, and he repeated to me that "Eastern capital got in on the fight to knock out the New Deal atmosphere that had grown up in Georgia."

Reaction in the South makes common cause with conservatism in the North; if this is not a cue for progressives in both sections to come together, then it means nothing.

A few weeks after the Monroe massacre I stood alone at the ancient, gnarled oak before which two Negro women and two Negro men were lined up and riddled with bullets. I admit to a feeling of sweaty fright as I glanced at the tree, then carefully all around at the spectral, hushed hollow. Four huge X-marks, each an inch deep and a foot high, had been carved into the trunk. Over this bold, fearsome sight hung an iron chain suspended from a steel spike. An iron ring dangled at the end of the chain. The whole thing was a Klan symbol.

I charge that state investigators are responsible for the stamping of this Klan imprint into that tree, and the hanging of that tortuous, defiant chain. The lynch spot was under constant surveillance for weeks after the killings and nobody could have approached it day or night without the state investigators' seeing them. It would have taken an hour alone to have carved the X-marks. That supremacist symbolism was knifed into the oak either with investigation men smilingly looking on, or, as I am convinced, by themselves.

Jim Crow America!

I have attempted to picture the more significant structures, currents, processes, movements, tendencies in what I choose to call *the system of Jim Crow,* an economic and political growth like fungus on the troubled tree of private enterprise. One cannot correctly view the "Negro" as an individual or group apart from the context of the entire national past. I have sought to indicate that just as there are broad social systems in the world called capitalism, communism, feudalism, fascism, colonialism, so Jim Crow is a broad social system unto itself while still integral to the private enterprise economy. The term "Jim Crow" signifies the institutions of discrimination, segregation, and prejudice. It connotes the responsibility of white, official America for the victimization of the colored in all spheres of living. It distinguishes the profits extractable from the Negro group as apart from income derivable from the rest of the national economy.

In the same way that slavery was a system and the rising industrial economy of the North a system, so too, in our time, the body politic of the Negro is an extraordinarily evolved and involved, constantly changing network of socio-economic patterns understandable only in light of the whole. Moreover, there can be no liberation for the Negro, no genuine effort in his behalf by himself alone or with allies, unless the need for a systemic campaign based upon the systemic scope of his condition is perceived.

In the same way that colonialism is integral to the economy of Great Britain and other countries, so too does the Negro represent a form of semi-colonialism within the framework of American economy. The special methods of housing, employing, educating,

[230

separating, ruling, controlling, and living with and apart from the Negro mass constitute a highly refined and historically evolved pattern, understandable only in a systemic concept.

The colonial comparison is borne out further in the fact that Negro Americans often act politically in the same way as the colonials. Colonials throughout the world have petitioned the United Nations Security Council for relief; so have the Negro Americans. As 1947 opened, a petition campaign initiated by the National Negro Congress to secure five million signatures urging "higher standards" for the Negro people was under way; the petition would go to the Human Rights Commission of the United Nations Security Council.

It should be clear that just as our nation has created a special nation in its own midst, just so surely has it invited the present forward-rolling motion of that mass and its allies now being felt in Washington and in each state capital. Three hundred years of exclusion of the Negro are operating now like the thrown rubber ball with the attached cord. Jim Crow is bouncing back in the face of an Uncle Sam who has historically tossed it outward. What will happen when the ball finally returns I do not know, but I do know that it is returning with company: labor, liberalism, and world colonial support.

The logic of resistance in the Negro is one which utilizes all the weaknesses in the economy, politics, philosophy, and religion of the dominant group. On the one hand, it drives the Negro to integrate himself as fully as possible into the broad national fabric, and on the other hand compels him to create a world of his own in his ghettos and in the areas of the South where he is massed. He builds his own economy, while battling to penetrate the white man's economy. He fights for realization as a national or mass group of his own, yet concurrently seeks to join the nation's mainstream. I find that both these processes are historical and inevitable, and not contradictory, inevitable to a greatly outnumbered group which must seek all methods of advance. The Negro aspires to full

231]

representation in government. That has one implication in the North and another in the South. In the North it means he wishes integration as a minority. In the South it means he is marching steadily toward something comparable to the position he had in the Reconstruction period, when Negroes constituted a majority in many Southern legislatures.

A century ago William Lloyd Garrison examined the Constitution and came to the conclusion that it was a pro-slavery document. This led him to the position that there was no hope for the Negro within that document, and he advanced his dis-unionist position. He said: "No union with slaveholders. Let us in the North dissociate from the South. Let them have their own country and their own social system; we cannot and will not have slavery. We will be a free North and a free country." It was a provocative position, not really conducive to freeing the Negro, but it could evoke great moral indignation about slavery. Other anti-slavers, including Frederick Douglass, interpreted the Constitution as an anti-slavery document and contended that it could be made to work in the interests of the Negro. Through the Constitution the Negro might be liberated. This resulted in the parliamentary struggle to stem the advance of slavery into the West. Finally, when the Civil War did come, there were present elements of both these philosophies. The South seceded and actually sought to set itself up as a nation of its own, with a slave system of its own. Meanwhile the logic of a parliamentary struggle brought Lincoln's government to grips with this Confederacy. When the war was ended the Confederacy was broken, the Union was restored, and the Constitution was increased by three amendments, each significant especially for the Negro. The Thirteenth abolished slavery and involuntary servitude; the Fourteenth guaranteed equal protection under the law and protection of life, liberty, and property; and the Fifteenth granted the right to vote to Negro men.

As the post-Civil War history of the nation advanced all the amendments were abridged for Negroes. Thousands were herded into peonage and sharecropping. The states of the South and the West reared black codes which the Supreme Court then sustained and now sustains, thus canceling the intent of the amendments. The poll tax came in later to deny the right to vote to four or five million Negroes and to an even greater number of whites. Such is the general condition in America today. The humane amendments have been nullified. In the course of their nullification for Negroes, whites too have suffered abridgment of their living and property privileges.

What this means is that, as in the time of Garrison, we are back to a position where we have to ask ourselves whether the Constitution is democratic or anti-democratic. Can the Negro, and indeed many others in class, national, religious, and other minority categories, achieve security and freedom within the framework of the Constitution as it now stands and as it has been interpreted by the Supreme Court? I believe that if Garrison were here today he would contend that the American failure to enforce the three amendments brought in after the Civil War condemns the Constitution as a document that has persisted in failure. Whether it can be made to work becomes therefore one of the major issues of the middle twentieth century.

It must be remembered that color prejudice was born and nurtured in America out of the womb of economic greed. It was *legislated into existence*. Discriminatory laws created prejudice. Enforcement of the laws drove the prejudice into the people's minds and ways. Then, generations of whites began to appear who accepted, without question, the status *created by law* for them, and, conversely, the status created for the Negro. By the same token, *legislation is a great part of the answer, and laws can erase prejudice, if enforced*.

In my *Defender* column I made the suggestion that the country could use a new "Human Rights Amendment" to the Constitution. This would be an amendment to make it a prison offense for any-

233]

one to slander, insult, or hold in contempt any other for "race," color, creed, religion, or national origin. The battle for such an amendment alone would heighten the understanding of millions and set people in motion.

Yet even if we did get rid of racism in the law, we would still have to eliminate it from the heart. The heart of it is in the whole historic-economic picture which I have attempted to paint. Only a new Reconstruction government in the South, such as was so evilly and forcibly taken away from the Negro and progressive whites in the 1870's, can strike at the heart of the evil in American institutions and men's minds.

The great needs of the Negro people North and South today are for land, jobs, freedom from segregated living conditions and institutions, and deliverance from caste indignity. They demand that all Jim Crow laws be repealed. They demand, require, and should secure full and even special representation in government, especially in the South where in many areas their majority ought to have a determining voice.

It seems to me that labor, liberals, and the interracial movement can strengthen themselves and the Negro enormously by throwing major forces into the battle against segregated housing, perhaps the greatest evil because it fathers so many of the secondary characteristics of prejudice and group animosity. The most stubborn resistance in America to Negro advance is offered by realtors and landholders. There may be as much profit-inspired prejudice and antagonism to the Negro on the board of directors of the Metropolitan Life Insurance Company, sponsors of the segregated Stuyvesant Town housing project in New York City, as one could find in an equal number of Southern senators. One of the most successful campaigns of all against the Negro issues, not from Richmond, Atlanta, or Birmingham, but from New York City and Chicago, from those who control the zoning of residential neighborhoods.

[234

JIM CROW CROSSROADS

An East Indian newspaper publisher visiting the United States discussed with me the condition of the Negro American and proposed the idea that the group might be powerful and numerous enough to apply economic sanctions to white America as a means of making known its oppression and its aspirations. He cited the effect and the success of Mahatma Gandhi in applying this principle to the British power, and I agreed with him that he "might have something." It is an interesting thought, worth the consideration of Negro, labor, and interracial organizations, and I pass it along here.

Despite all I have said about the tremendous strictures placed upon the Negro in all areas of life, about the compromise, active antagonism, ignorance, darkness, viciousness, and brutality that ravage our subverted democracy, I have also indicated that great modern "Jim Crow abolitionist" forces are working even in the heart of the major political parties. Stalwart men like former Governor Ellis Arnall of Georgia and Senator Claude Pepper of Florida, and organizations such as the Southern Conference for Human Welfare, have helped restore some reason and decency to an historically deceived, brutalized, and pathetic portion of the land. There are stout hearts now that speak in the obscurest parts of "Darkest America." There is Homer Rainey in Texas, and "Joan of Arc" Polly Dobbs in Birmingham. The great leavening force of *labor organization* is digging the foundation for a new deal in the South. Here and there the Negro has again taken hold of the ballot. His rights in the courts secure at least a modicum of respect beyond what was accorded a few years ago. An upswing of Klan brutality against the black man is an inverse indication of the strides being made by Negro and white alliance. The white South grows more and more concerned over Northern criticism. The Southern church stares itself in the face these days, and some segments covertly work with progress as much as they dare while Christianity remains under the wing of the plantation economy. Senator Bilbo returns to office to sing like a mocking bird a chorus of prejudice for the whole world to hear. Everywhere the contradictions intensify and the Negro sees rays of new hope striking upon him. As the "One World" concept merges with the "Century of the Common Man" idea, the Negro American sees the issue of his welfare returning to the van of national life.

Even as the Jew has been the conscience of Europe in the recent period, so the Negro has emerged as the conscience of the United States.

Let America ignore this question, or further compromise it, and it is my sober prediction that Jim Crow will break the back of free enterprise and the system of individualism just as a century ago the Negro question tore the states apart.

The Garrisonian impulses were moralistic. In our day it is clear that not only must moral values of human freedom be taken into account but overwhelmingly no new "morality" can obtain save that it inhere in all of society's struggle for a more secure society. Today's "Garrisonians" are the great hosts of labor, who must act, with all other forces of advance in the Negro's behalf, if even only in enlightened self-interest. More and more segments of white America must and will be thrown into motion on this issue. It is time for the formation of a kind of "Committee of White Allies," or a "Committee for Negro Liberation," dedicated to the main object of integrating the Negro's cause with the whole national and world cause of freedom and anti-fascism. The phalanx of white friends of the Negro, although operating in labor, church, business, and other spheres, needs now to be brought into a great special camp, with the driving fervor of the old abolitionist movement at its helm. Such a force must be inevitably allied with all those great Franklin D. Roosevelt dreams, motives, and practicalities which are by no means dead in America but waiting the press of the right buttons to swing once more into motion. The right "button," that which has historically and inevitably been dynamic in America, is white enlistment in behalf of the Negro. Such impulses would be linked inextricably with the great groping force, shattered since the

[236

close of the war, that wants increased justice for all Americans. The Wallace ideal and the reorganization of the coalition of the dispossessed, the struggling, the honest, the "plain people," the minorities, the liberal Republicans and Democrats—all these must and will gather together and go forward to a higher society. Only when it is recognized that the Negro is the touchstone and root and link to all American progress can progress's pendulum swing upward again in America as it is doing in so many other parts of the world. Make no mistake: the Negro will *win* freedom. With or without aid he will strike his blows in his own behalf, and automatically in behalf of all who seek a better life: but it were better if millions of whites, who really hold the key to Negro advance in America, moved in the Negro's behalf and alongside the Negro.

I know that Negro liberation is inevitable as I know that ultimately the liberation of all the people in the world is inevitable, for I know that the struggle for economic and political security is now a world institution.

Our country, historical land of democratic principles, must make the decision to vanquish racism. From 1776 until 1861, and up to our participation in the struggle against fascism, and to the current domestic issue of racist reaction versus democratic and ethnic advance, the people's liberation drive has continued. At the hub of this broad conflict is the same issue around which the American political wheel has always revolved—the economic-political-moral issue of Negro rights. This issue is pivotal; it is all-contingent; it is decisive. If a major task of progress a century ago was the abolition of chattel slavery, there can be no doubt that in the present hour a comparably immense objective is the abolition of the institutions of discrimination, legalized prejudice, and barriers to national group understanding. America cannot be a free land and at the same time the land of Jim Crow.